Teaching Health Law: A Guide on Health Law for Health Services Administration

Edited by

Arnold J. Rosoff, J.D.
The University of Pennsylvania

and

David F. Bergwall, D.B.A.
AUPHA

Task Force on Health Law

Association of University Programs in Health Administration

1911 North Fort Myer Drive
Suite 503
Arlington, Virginia 22209

The preparation and publication of this book
was made possible by a grant from the
Pew Memorial Trust

Copyright 1986 by
Association of University Programs in Health Administration,
1911 North Fort Myer Drive, Suite 503
Arlington, Virginia 22209.

Library of Congress Catalog Card No. 86-073246

ISBN 0-910591-01-6

Contents

Preface		vii
1.	Introduction	1
	What Is Unique and Special About Teaching Health Law?	3
	Why Is a Health Law Task Force Needed?	5
	The Work of the Task Force	6
	How To Use This Guide	8
2.	Integration of Health Care Law Into the Health Administration Program	11
	The Nature of Programs	13
	Table 2-1 Career Destinations of Health Services Administration Students	18
	The Role and Responsibilities of the Program Director	19
	Toward a Managed Curriculum	27
3.	Teaching Objectives and Methods	29
	Environment	30
	Objectives	35
	Table 3-1 Objectives of Health Law Teachers (Survey Results)	36
	Methods	39
	Table 3-2 Methods for Teaching Health Law (Survey Results)	40
	Table 3-3 Teaching Techniques Used by Health Law Teachers (Survey Results)	41
	Evaluation	50
	Grading	53
	Conclusion	54
4.	Content of Graduate Health Law Courses	55
	Settings	55
	Program Outcomes	59

	Purposes and Objectives of Instruction in Health Law	65
	Content of Graduate Courses in Health Law	68
	Example Courses	76
5.	Baccalaureate Programs in Health Administration: Health Law Education	87
	Objectives and Content of Health Law	90
	Methods	94
	Attachment I: Position Description of Respondents Currently Employed in Health	98
	Attachment II: Primary Areas of Responsibility and Activities/Tasks for Respondents Currently Employed in the Health Field	99
	Attachment III: Knowledge and Skill Areas	100
6.	Teaching Materials	105
	Use of Textbooks versus Bulkpack Materials	105
	Copyright Issues	114
	Use of the Law Library	115
	Summary	116
	Selected List of Teaching Materials	117
7.	Dealing With Lawyers in a Health Care Setting	119
	Making the Lawyer-Client Relationship Work	119
	Using Lawyers Effectively	127
	The Role of Inside Counsel	134
	Teaching Prospective Health Administrators How To Work With Lawyers	137
	The Value of Teaching Legal Fundamentals	138
	Possible Teaching Approaches	139
	Incentives for Participation By Practitioners	143

8.	Continuing Education for Health Law Teachers	145
	Health Law Professional Organizations	146
	American Academy of Hospital Attorneys	147
	American Bar Association	149
	American College of Legal Medicine	150
	American Society of Law and Medicine	153
	National Health Lawyers Association	156
	Workshops, Symposia and Conferences	159
	Health Law Publications	161
	The Health Law Teacher's Role in Continuing Education	165
	Appendix: Other Publications of Interest to Health Law Teachers	166
9.	Health Law Course Outlines	169
Appendix: Bibliography from the *Journal of Health Politics, Policy and Law*		199

PREFACE

Teaching Health Law: A Guide on Health Law for Health Services Administration was developed by the Association of University Programs in Health Administration (AUPHA) Health Law Task Force. The activities of the task force were funded over a three-year period from the Pew Memorial Trust, which supported not only this task force but a related effort on Ethics and Health Management, as well as general curriculum development for AUPHA.

Health administration education is multidisciplinary in structure and content. The building blocks of the professional curriculum reside in a number of disciplines, including public health, medicine, management, political science, law, and their academic subject areas. AUPHA provides leadership to the consortium of its members in melding and shaping the content of these areas into health management curricula.

Assisting universities in curricular development is AUPHA's highest priority. It has conducted a number of highly successful curriculum projects that have significantly altered the scope, content, and quality of health administration education. Previous efforts were primarily responsible for shifting the curriculum from descriptive institutional management to a systemwide analytic approach. Other endeavors led to much greater emphasis on the development of quantitative skills, financial management, and planning. The present activity adds still another dimension to curricular development by addressing the relationship of law to the management of health services delivery.

In 1980 a small group of health law teachers began working informally to address these issues. In 1983 AUPHA officially convened a task force to address issues in the teaching of health law in health administration programs. Support by the Pew Memorial Trust made it possible for the efforts of this task force to be consolidated and for this guide to be produced. Broadly stated, the mission of the AUPHA Health Law Task Force was to provide support to improve the quality of health law teaching in AUPHA member health services administration programs. The task force was charged with the following specific objectives:

1. To provide up-to-date guidance on the scope and content of health law for health administration education and practice;
2. To identify, assemble, and develop needed teaching resources to enhance the breadth and quality of health law teaching;
3. To explore and assess nontraditional approaches to meeting the legal education needs of the field;
4. To identify and establish AUPHA's continuing role in relation to health law in the teaching process.

Health law faculty, practitioners, and a director from a health administration education program contributed to this effort. The members of the Health Law Task Force were Arnold J. Rosoff, J.D. (Chair), The Wharton School, University of Pennsylvania; David G. Warren, J.D. (Vice-Chair), Duke University Medical Center; David F. Bergwall, D.B.A., AUPHA; Darryl E. Crompton, J.D., University of Alabama, Birmingham; Mary Jane Dundas, J.D., Arizona State University; Robert L. McNair, Esq., Wolf, Block, Schorr & Solis-Cohen, Philadelphia, Pennsylvania; Eugene S. Schneller, Ph.D., Arizona State University; Arthur F. Southwick, J.D., University of Michigan; and Michael L. Ziegler, Esq., Epstein, Becker, Borsody & Green, New York, New York. Several other individuals contributed to the process through review or writing of materials. In particular, Eileen A. O'Neil, J.D., University of New Hampshire, contributed her thoughts on undergraduate education, and Wendy K. Mariner, J.D., provided the perspective of the Health Law Teachers Section of the American Society of Law and Medicine, which was most helpful in its efforts on this subject.

The Task Force process was one of collegial debate and discourse, with individual positions, for the most part, ultimately merging into a group view. This present publication, then, is put forward as the product of the group as a whole. In the drafting process, however, individual members took principal responsibility for the various chapters as follows: Introduction (ch. 1), Arnold J. Rosoff; Integration of Health Law Into the Health Administration Program (ch. 2), Eugene S. Schneller; Teaching Objectives and Methods (ch. 3), David G. Warren; Content of Graduate Health Law Courses (ch. 4), Arthur F. Southwick; Content of Baccalaureate Health Law Courses (ch. 5), Eileen A. O'Neil; Teaching Materials (ch. 6), Mary Jane Dundas; How Health Administrators Relate to Lawyers (ch. 7), Robert M. McNair; and Continuing Education for the Health Law Teacher (ch. 8), Darryl E. Crompton.

We offer this Curriculum Guide not as a prescriptive structure for the field of health administration but as an aid for curricular development in various university settings in which health administration and health law are taught.

Arnold J. Rosoff, J.D.
David F. Bergwall, D.B.A.
December 1986

CHAPTER 1

INTRODUCTION

Practitioners and educators in the health administration field have increasingly come to appreciate the importance of law as a major force affecting the delivery of health care services. As a result, a number of the core disciplines of health administration programs now embrace elements of legal and government processes and devote some attention to the skills of legal reasoning and public policy analysis. While organizational design and financial management are particularly important interfaces with the law, there are many others as well.

Most programs in health administration have long included some health law content. Two distinct legal focuses have characterized the programs, depending on whether they emphasize institutional management or public health. In both cases, though, teaching of the law tended to be narrowly focused on specific applications and geared to the level thought appropriate to the needs of administrators in day-to-day management. The law content was usually contained in an omnibus course designed to cover topics "left over" from the principal curriculum. This level of commitment to coverage of the law has changed gradually, leading to a formal recognition of the importance of health law as an academic subject and, ultimately, to the development of the AUPHA Health Law Task Force.

In 1982, the heightened awareness of the importance of the law to health administration was formalized by the inclusion of a "health law content" requirement in the accrediting standards of the Accrediting Commission on Education for Health Services Administration (ACEHSA). Consistent with the vagueness with which this requirement is defined, there is a great deal of variability among the health law offerings of the various AUPHA member programs. This variability manifests itself in course content and materials; length of courses; number and mix of students; teaching objectives, approaches and methods; required versus optional nature of the course(s); background, qualifications and orientation of the instructor(s); integration of the instructor(s) into the health administration program; and status of the instructor(s) among faculty peers. Much of this variability is deliberately correlated with differences among the various health administration programs; thus, for the most part, the diversity is positive. Each program must stand largely on its own and be evaluated in terms of its own unique setting, resources, and goals.

Some of the observed diversity is not positive, however. The change in the legal environment of health services delivery has far outpaced the scope, content, and rigor of legal education for the field. The programs have responded in uneven ways to the increased need for legal education. Some appear to have seriously underestimated the need of the contemporary health administrator for knowledge of the law, while others have provided substantial coverage of legal materials, anticipating a future environment of even greater legal complexity. Obviously, there is a lack of consensus among educators and practitioners as to what is needed. This is compounded by a lack of appropriate teaching materials and properly equipped faculty. Only a limited number of health administration programs have had the luxury of full-time health law faculty. The predominant model for including health law content in the programs has been the use of a part-time, or adjunct, faculty member who is a practicing lawyer in the local community. The lack of training and experience in pedagogy that such faculty typically reflect has further contributed to the unevenness of legal content in health administration program curricula.

It is not the intention of the task force to prescribe a fixed, or "lock-step," approach to the teaching of health law in health administration programs. Still, the task force's inquiry into the way health law is currently being taught suggests that not all the variability observed is the result of deliberate, informed choice. Instructors are searching for the optimal way to impart a knowledge of health law to health administration students. Thus, the principal objective of the task force is to provide support to the programs and faculty seeking to enhance their effectiveness in this highly important area.

WHAT IS UNIQUE AND SPECIAL ABOUT TEACHING HEALTH LAW?

Although the subject of health law has much in common with other content areas in the health administration curriculum, it also has some important differences. In the first place, students of health administration often do not have the same level of basic knowledge of law as they are expected to have--and generally do have--of other subjects in the curriculum, such as health care systems organization, management structures, and financing arrangements. Many students enter health administration programs with a working background in the health care system and have had firsthand experience with many of the subjects that constitute the health administration curriculum. In fact, many students may have had exposure to legal issues too, but rarely in a direct, "hands-on" context such as would allow intimate involvement with and full understanding of these issues.

Health law faculty also tend to differ somewhat from other health administration faculty. Their educational background and orientation generally involve an applied, professional education and a J.D. degree rather than a research and education focus as expressed through a doctoral degree. Consequently, these individuals may not approach their teaching mission in the same way as other faculty members. Compounding this difference, many health law faculty are not full-time academics. Adjunct faculty have a very different academic life-style and may experience difficulty in becoming integrated into the overall program. Generally this difficulty does not rise to the level of a problem, but it is a significant factor that should be considered in managing the health administration curriculum and program.

It may also be--although this is not universally acknowledged--that health administration students have a different educational objective when approaching health law subjects. When in their careers they are called on to apply their knowledge of health law subjects, they will often do so through, or in conjunction with, a lawyer-- a professional who presumably will understand the subject matter in much greater depth than they do. A manager's involvement with other types of issues (finance, marketing, personnel, and employee relations) is more direct. Understanding a subject for the purpose of dealing with it indirectly is a different matter from understanding it in order to deal with it directly and substantively. If, in fact, the student's application of health law knowledge is going to be significantly different, as the task force believes, this would seem to call for a different educational approach.

Closely related to this last point, there may be wider variance in beliefs as to what students in health administration programs need to know about health law than there is with regard to other subjects in the curriculum. This difference in perception may occur among the students, the faculty, or both. Faculty in more traditional health administration areas may view law, which they perceive as a "latecomer," as peripheral, optional, or even largely irrelevant. Students, too, may have an initial impression that the legal materials are less pertinent than other subjects in the health administration curriculum. Such perception on the part of faculty and students may both lead to and stem from the fact that health law is less likely to be a required part of the health administration program than are many other subjects. In some cases, it may be more difficult for health law to gain and maintain its rightful status in the overall program curriculum. The task force has not observed any direct evidence of this undervaluing of health law as a subject, but we are concerned, nonetheless, that it may exist. The possibility should be recognized and appropriate steps taken to counter it.

One thing favoring the position of health law in the health administration curriculum is that students tend to find the legal materials intrinsically interesting. They welcome the change of pace, both in terms of content and educational approach, that the health law course offers. The inherent appeal of the course may make it somewhat easier to teach. On the other hand, this factor could mask deficiencies in teaching that would otherwise be more readily detectable. Health law teachers might be able to engage students and maintain their interest without providing the well-balanced educational substance necessary to prepare them for what they will encounter in their careers. This possibility puts a special burden on health law teachers and health administration program directors to ensure that the teaching in this area is of consistently high quality.

WHY IS A HEALTH LAW TASK FORCE NEEDED?

Why, one might ask, is a task force on health law teaching needed? The question has many answers. As noted above, the task force has perceived that there is substantial variability in health law teaching among AUPHA member programs. Just as nature abhors a vacuum, academics cannot resist exploring the differences they observe in other academics' educational approaches. Without meaning to trivialize our endeavor or motivations, we candidly admit that we were driven in part by academic curiosity to learn what exists and why. But there were other, more practical, motivations as well.

Most of us have, over the years, been contacted on occasion by people or programs seeking help in designing or upgrading their health law courses. We have generally responded individually to requests for syllabi, reading lists, pedagogic tips, and the like; but all of us have wished that there were a comprehensive reference source to which we could direct such inquiries, either in lieu of or in addition to what we could individually provide. The greater prevalence of part-time faculty in health law means that more faculty in this field are likely to want help in curriculum development, course design, identification of course materials, teaching methods, and so on. Thus, while we believe educational task forces and curriculum guides are useful in any discipline, we think there is a special need for such assistance in the field of health law.

Other factors also deserve recognition. First, the fast-moving nature of the health law field makes it harder to keep courses and materials up-to-date. Consequently, faculty--even full-time faculty--can use more help in this area. Second, as a relative newcomer to the health administration field, health law needs more help in getting established. Collegial cooperation obviously works toward filling this need. Third, as already noted, the nature of health law, which involves managers in dealing with another, "foreign" profession, requires a different educational approach for adequate preparation.

There is some danger that the optimal approach may not be the one naturally followed in health law teaching. Rather, many health law teachers may simply adopt law school teaching methodology and objectives, mimicking an approach that has much to commend it but that may, at the least, need to be modified for this new application. While we do not, as a group, hold a single, unified idea of what is "the right way" to teach health law, we do uniformly believe that each teacher must choose his or her approach by thoughtful, informed deliberation, not simply by inadvertence or by assuming a consensus on methods that does not, in fact, exist.

While health law teachers are the primary audience for which we produced this guide, we hope that program directors and other faculty will study it in order to achieve an increased understanding of the mission, approaches, and contributions of health law teachers to health administration curricula and programs.

THE WORK OF THE TASK FORCE

The history and composition of the task force were discussed in the Preface to this guide. Once the group was convened, we turned our attention to defining objectives and developing a work plan. One of the first and most important elements of that plan was to conduct a survey of health law faculty to discover (1) the current status of health law teaching, (2) what needs existed that the task force might help to satisfy, (3) how our contribution might best be structured, and (4) whether there were others outside the task force who would be interested and willing to help in its work.

On this last point, it was most fortunate that, at about the time we were beginning our work, the American Society of Law and Medicine (ASLM) convened a Health Law Teachers Section to work on a similar project. [See *Law, Medicine and Health Care*, September 1983, 10(4):175.] The principal difference between the two groups was that our task force was focused specifically on health administration programs, faculty, and students. The ASLM group had a much broader charge that included the teaching of health law in schools of law, medicine, public health, allied health professions, and the like. For this reason, it also had a broader range of participants. However, the work of the two organizations meshed nicely and, with the help of ASLM's then Executive Director, A. Edward Doudera, and the ASLM Task Force Chairperson, Wendy K. Mariner, a useful and satisfying collaboration was established and maintained.

The Health Law Teacher Survey in health administration programs, conducted in the spring of 1984, yielded some very interesting information that has been used as the basis for much of our deliberation and is reflected throughout this report. The surveying process was intended not only to gather information, but to make health administration programs and health law teachers aware of the efforts of the task force.

The bulk of the task force's work consisted of meeting to discuss various aspects of health law teaching--basically the range of subjects covered in this guide. Various members of the task force took primary responsibility for particular subject areas and prepared discussion outlines that were reviewed by other members, debated, revised, and then debated again. This interactive process was time-consuming and not without its tensions and frustrations, but eventually the group was able to form a consensus on most substantive issues. Prime values of the task force were the maintenance of a forum in which these issues could be discussed in detail and a commitment to making a contribution in this field of education.

At various stages in the process, the group presented progress reports on its work to outside groups and individuals. Much emphasis was placed on getting input from others not directly involved in the task force's work. In the final stages of the work period, we pulled together a tentative draft of this guide and prsented it for discussion at the AUPHA 1986 Annual Meeting. The document that we now present for your consideration is a refinement of that draft.

HOW TO USE THIS GUIDE

This guide has been written for a dual audience. Principally intended for health law teachers, it is also aimed at directors of health administration programs, who have the very important job of seeing that health law content is effectively integrated into the overall program curriculum. Chapter 2, "Integration of Health Care Law Into the Health Administration Program," speaks to the issues of coordination and integration and should be of particular interest to program directors.

Chapter 3, "Teaching Objectives and Methods," Chapter 4, "Content of Graduate Health Law Courses," and Chapter 5, "Baccalaureate Programs in Health Administration:Health Law Education," form the backbone of the guide. These three chapters are strongly oriented toward the health law teacher, although they, too, should make useful reading for program directors. Chapter 6, "Teaching Materials," covers some of the literature available to the health law teacher.

Chapter 7, "Dealing With Lawyers in a Health Care Setting," recognizes the fact that health care managers will usually deal with legal issues in conjunction with legal counsel. This interaction between manager and lawyer is subtle and sensitive and often takes effort and expertise to work optimally. Chapter 7 deals with both the substance of this interaction and also the process of teaching this subject matter to health administration students. Robert M. McNair, a practicing lawyer with considerable experience in working with health care managers, was the prime contributor to this chapter.

Chapter 8, "Continuing Education for Health Law Teachers," supplies important information on professional organizations and activities of use to health lawyers and those who teach in this field. Teaching a successful course involves the challenging task of staying up-to-date in a fast-changing substantive field. Educational activities and resources accessible through the organizations identified and described in this chapter can help tremendously in this endeavor.

In approaching the material contained in this guide, one must remember that it was never intended as a "cookbook." Rather, it is the starting point for individual thought and for dialogue between the various people--most notably the health law teacher and the health administration program director--who share responsibility for the success of health law teaching. Our purpose throughout has been to ensure that health law is properly integrated into the overall health administration curriculum. This cannot be accomplished by the health law teacher alone; it also takes the participation, understanding, and support of others. We strongly hope that this guide can be of significant assistance to that undertaking.

CHAPTER 2

INTEGRATION OF HEALTH CARE LAW
INTO THE HEALTH ADMINISTRATION PROGRAM

The modern health care administrator requires skills and knowledge in a variety of management and industry specific areas. Health care law is one such area. Discussions with program directors reveal an increased understanding of the importance of the legal environment, appreciation of the law, and recognition of the complexities and problems involved in providing students with the most important and useful information.

Reflecting the apparent consensus over including health law in the curriculum, the task force survey found that a specific course in health law is required in 58 percent of the graduate programs. In another 15 percent of the graduate programs, a health care law course is included among the defined list of courses from which students must choose (that is, a semi-elective, or "bracket," requirement).

Overall, it appears that roughly 75 percent of the graduate health administration programs expose most of their students to "health law content" in a separate course prior to graduation. Health law content may also appropriately appear in courses other than health care law, including labor relations, hospital organization, health planning, and health policy. Some students are exposed to health care law issues in their field training as residents and interns, but the extent to which such exposure is built into residency and internship plans was not explored in our questionnaire.

Integration of the health care law content into the overall curriculum, however, requires serious attention. Fewer than half of the health law teachers responding to the survey reported attending faculty meetings "often," and fewer than 60 percent believed that the course they teach is well-integrated into the curriculum. Since more than 32 percent of the respondents teach in a health administration program only part time (51 percent reporting that they are practitioners with none located in a unit of the university other than the health administration program), it is unlikely that such faculty will have an opportunity to influence their program's curriculum design or even be able to assess fully the contribution made by their course to the overall curriculum. This report explores the relationship between the curriculum of the health administration program and its health law component, with special emphasis on curriculum integration.

If, as Arthur Southwick has argued, "virtually all substantive and procedural subject matter areas of the law--an entire three year law school curriculum and more --have an impact upon the delivery and financing of health care," the task of selecting carefully those topic areas most relevant to the objectives of the course, the career goals of the students, the maturity and academic level of the students, and the educational mission of the program in which the course or courses are taught, is, to say the least, difficult. For both the program director, working to balance the program's curriculum to achieve its goals, and the health law teachers, who often report that the programs place too little emphasis on health law, a rational, articulated process for curriculum design is desirable. Given demands for more time in the curriculum by those representing the functional areas of management and the other health services administration specialties involved in training future health care administrators, it is most likely that the "optimal" curriculum in law, as in the other areas, will give way to a negotiated apportionment of time.

It is the role of the program director to ensure curricular balance. In light of the low level of routine input and influence of the health care law teacher in programs, it is important to avoid a health care law component that is developed by "default." The following discussion of program management for curriculum design is ordered to reflect some of the essential features of the milieu of the health law course:

1. The heterogeneous environment of programs in health administration. This recognizes the various goals and ideologies of programs as they relate to curricular process and politics in the schools in which they are housed.

2. The heterogeneity reported to exist in courses in health care law, including course duration, goals, and student composition.

3. The variety of student career outcomes observed for programs in health administration.

4. The characteristics of the health law teacher and the relationships between the teacher and the program director and other faculty.

The discussion of the role of the program director in course design, evaluation, coordination, and the selection of faculty is aimed at the program director and the health law teacher. The implications of our survey findings and argument for a "managed" health law component in the overall program curriculum constitute the last section of the chapter. Although many of the issues raised are generic to program management, the health law content, we believe, is especially vulnerable in negotiations concerning curriculum design and development, perhaps necessitating a "protected species" status.

THE NATURE OF PROGRAMS

The Heterogeneous Environment of Health Administration Programs

Settings. Graduate and undergraduate programs in health administration are located in a variety of settings (colleges and schools) within the broader university community, including business administration, management, public health, medicine, public administration, community and family medicine, and allied health. Degrees at the graduate level include the M.B.A., M.P.H., M.S., M.H.A., M.H.S.A., and perhaps others. The colleges and schools in which programs are located have undergone significant change over time and are affected by a variety of forces both within and beyond their control. In some instances, programs in health administration have moved from one school to another or "merged" with other schools by offering joint or concurrent degrees (e.g., M.B.A./M.H.S.A.). A number of programs cooperate in concurrent undergraduate and graduate programs.

Over the last two decades, school accreditation criteria and standards have influenced decisions made about the resources allocated in schools of business and public health. The goals of health administration programs have not always been viewed as central or compatible by college administrators who focus on the "broader picture." Thus, the amount of negotiation involved in developing and maintaining a curriculum has increased, which obviously adds to the complexity of implementing program goals.

Goals. Given the diversity of the settings in which programs are located, it is not surprising that programs articulate a wide variety of statements regarding the level of employment anticipated for graduates, eventual career destinations for graduates, and target roles in various types of organizations.

The following statements, taken from *Health Services Administration Education* (AUPHA, 1985-87, Arlington, Va.) indicate the range of diversity.

Undergraduate Statements:

"To prepare soundly trained health care administrators with a business orientation."

"The bachelor's degree program stresses the basic administrative principles and skills required for entry-level positions in health care administration and provides the theoretical foundation for applicants to the master's degree program in health administration."

"The program is designed to upgrade the knowledge and skills of those already working in the field of health services administration and to provide those with two-year degrees the opportunity to complete a baccalaureate program."

"To prepare first-line and some middle-level health care managers for functioning as beginning practitioners in hospitals, nursing homes, health maintenance organizations, and other private, public, and voluntary health agencies."

Graduate Statements:

"A problem-solving, decision-making thrust within a generalist, practitioner-focused philosophy of health services administration."

"A thorough knowledge of the managerial tenets and techniques fundamental to the effective administration of health care delivery, with particular emphasis on the federal sector."

"A distinct service and public sector orientation."

"Leadership positions in a wide variety of other health and health-related facilities."

"Oriented toward students with significant prior health field experience, and nearly all of the students in the program are currently employed in health professions and attending the program part time."

"The master's program is designed for individuals who seek executive positions in health organizations."

"To prepare individuals for careers in health policy or health administration."

"Preparing students for career mobility."

General education has emerged as an important issue for undergraduate education in the United States. The extent to which the mandate for general education will lead to a reduction of classroom time available for "professional" education is of concern to program directors. In settings where the potential conflict between these perspectives remains unresolved, courses such as health care law may be under pressure to achieve a large variety of objectives, including the broadening of the student's understanding of the American legal system, improvement of the student's general reasoning skills, development of the student's writing skills, and communication of knowledge from disciplines such as political science.

Student Profiles. Health administration programs recruit students with a wide range of educational backgrounds and abilities. Some 73 percent of the graduate programs are characterized by having predominantly full-time students (over 75 percent full time), with 72 percent of the undergraduate programs characterized by full-time enrollment. Many programs remain highly selective, with graduate programs accepting as few as 11 percent of their applicants and undergraduate programs as few as 14 percent. Others accept as many as 100 percent for both graduate and undergraduate programs. Some geographic locations in the United States are characterized by fierce competition for students. In the New York metropolitan area, for example, as many as seven programs, accredited and not accredited, seek to recruit students with career goals in health services administration.

The current situation, however, will undergo significant change over the coming decades. In an important study of the demographics of education, Harold L. Hodgkinson points out that "as the number of high school graduates declines more steeply from now to 1994, and fewer students are spread across the same number of institutions, the commendable specificity of college catalogues and brochures may be lost, as some institutions try to attract anyone who is warm and breathing to their opening class."

Education for health services administration will not be immune from such pressures. As the demographics of the American population change, programs will be forced to rethink their attitudes about full-time versus part-time students, students with no experience versus students with much relevant work experience, and "nontraditional" students. Shifts in the minority population and the implementation of college-wide affirmative action goals have important implications for future program selection procedures. In planning and redesigning curriculum, therefore, an understanding of the student/client of the future is necessary.

Student Outcomes

Initial employment of graduates. Programs in health services administration may be classified by the job outcomes of their students. Such outcomes are not, of course, always consistent with the program's stated goals. Students with aspirations different from the major focus of the program may choose a program on the basis of its geographic location, hoping that their degrees will be seen as sufficiently applicable to the broader industry. Indeed, a review of the variety of student outcomes from individual programs would suggest the complexities involved in the design and development of a health care law course to meet the goals of the employment marketplace. Table 2-1, generated from a recent AUPHA survey of health administration program graduates, reveals that graduates from undergraduate and master's level programs find initial employment in a wide variety of settings including hospitals, health maintenance organizations, health departments, regulatory agencies, consulting firms, nursing homes, and the insurance industry.

The differences in outcomes for undergraduate versus graduate programs is discussed in greater detail in Chapters

TABLE 2-1

Career Destinations of Health Services Administration Students

	Master's Level Number	Percent	Undergraduate Level Number	Percent
First Job				
Hospital	363	49.7	90	34.7
HMO	37	5.1	23	8.9
Group Practice	13	1.8	10	3.9
Health Department	6	.8	3	1.2
Nursing Home	22	3.0	28	10.8

SOURCE: *AUPHA 1985 Survey of Health Administration Student's First Post-Graduate Employment.*

4 and 5. It is noteworthy here that undergraduate programs enroll many "nontraditional" students. These individuals are often older than their counterparts in graduate school and are seeking credentialing to meet the entry requirements for the long-term-care sector and other parts of the healthcare industry not yet intent on the recruitment of master's-level graduates. Other undergraduate programs focus on the education of recent high school graduates. This heterogeneity in program goals and populations demands that curriculum development be customized by programs at the undergraduate as well as the graduate level.

Of course, long-range career outcomes are not always a function of the program one attends or one's initial setting of employment. Many senior managers in the 1980s are experiencing career dislocations into parts of the industry they never anticipated. In many instances, the settings in which they are employed did not even exist at the time they trained for the field. The extent to which the teaching of health care law should be geared to the immediate versus the eventual, the targeted versus the actual, and to desired versus undesired career outcomes of graduates is a topic for serious debate within programs. And the debate need not be limited to content in health care law.

Members of the task force agreed that while some content should be focused at the immediate career outcome(s) specified in the particular program's objectives, there are general lessons that apply to a broad range of settings in which program graduates will ultimately find themselves. From a course design perspective, it is important for the health care law teacher and program director to identify some of the "commonalities" of outcomes ensuring a "base level" of knowledge. This level was not readily identified by the members of the task force, however.

THE ROLE AND RESPONSIBILITIES OF THE PROGRAM DIRECTOR

The program director, in light of the variation within and among programs, is faced with the difficult task of recruiting and selecting a health care law teacher and working to integrate health care law into the curriculum. Program directors are concerned not only with information specific to health care, but also, given the operating environment in the health care industry, with the more general areas of legal knowledge. The transmission of legal information may not revolve only around the health care law course; but the health care law course does serve as the major building block for law content. And the program director, who typically has little training in law, will rely heavily on the individual chosen to teach the health law course. It is noteworthy that, so far as the members of the task force know, there are no program directors who have had formal training in law.

The differences in backgrounds between program directors and health law teachers may pose problems in choosing course content and achieving integration. Many directors actively practice--often as consultants, read relevant journals, and are aware of current medical/legal issues; but still their exposure is rarely systematic or sufficiently in-depth to provide them with a deeper understanding of the broad array of problems requiring legal input. Thus, the role of the program director is an important managerial one that must include:

1. Negotiating/communicating program goals to the health law teacher.

2. Recognizing the range of topics to be covered in the core law course and ensuring that what is not covered in that course is presented elsewhere.

3. Facilitating meetings between the law teacher and teachers in other courses where there is related content (for example, labor relations). Overlap is not necessarily to be avoided entirely; but it should exist, wherever possible, by design and not by oversight.

4. Encouraging continuing education. Given the wide variety of issues to be covered in the health care law course as well as the proliferation of information in the field, the program director is important in encouraging and facilitating the health care law teacher's attendance at meetings with colleague health care law teachers. Perhaps equally significant, the program director can provide the health care law teacher with the opportunity to attend meetings relating to the broader issues in the field of health services administration. Those health care law teachers who have attended the meetings of groups such as the American Public Health Association and the annual meetings of the Association of University Programs in Health Administration report gaining important perspective as a result of the experience.

5. Providing feedback by evaluating the course and the teacher. The evaluation of full-time and adjunct faculty is very difficult. There is the need to ensure that students give feedback on teaching, both in terms of the

appropriateness of the course materials and the ability of the instructor to communicate information. The uniqueness of health law content and the methods of teaching it bear on student evaluations of a teacher's performance, but it is not clear whether the effect is positive or negative.

Diversity Among Health Care Law Teachers

We have argued that the achievement of program goals requires the fine-tuning of curricular content within the broader context of program offerings. The program director, in selecting and interacting with a health care lawyer, must recognize that there is great diversity among those lawyers professing an interest in teaching health law.

Before profiling the respondents to the survey, we should note that a sizable portion of health care law teachers did not respond. In many instances we were not aware of the directions in which the responses were biased. According to the survey, for example, the typical health law instructor has been teaching for only three years. To understand the implications of this fully, we would need to know the extent to which respondents were from relatively new programs or programs experiencing a high turnover of dissatisfied health care law teachers.

Education. Of the survey's respondents, 85 percent reported having a law degree and 73 percent reported being licensed to practice law.

Full- versus part-time teachers. Few program directors, in meeting the staffing requirements for a comprehensive curriculum in health services administration, view the health care lawyer as a priority full-time resource. Only 58 percent of the respondents are full-time faculty members in the university in which the program is located. Those who are not full-time academics are engaged in legal practice (20 percent), the health insurance industry (17 percent), consulting work (8 percent), and a variety of other settings. Sixty-one percent of the respondents have primary appointments in the health administration program in which they are teaching, 5 percent have primary appointments in the law school, 10 percent in the business school, and 10 percent in the medical school.

Activity assessment. Of the full-time faculty members surveyed, the majority spend less than half of their time in course instruction. Eighty-three percent of the respondents teach one course in the health administration program, and 46 percent supply legal content, in undefined amounts to other program courses. The survey did not reveal whether the teaching loads of the respondents reflected the norm within the schools or, rather, a special arrangement between the university and the attorney.

None of the respondents reported substantial research, academic administration, or community service. Many are involved in the practice of law and/or consulting as their principal time allocation. In this respect, health law teachers differ significantly from their nonlawyer faculty counterparts. Although the survey questionnaire was not designed to explore the implications of this difference, we would expect that the application of conventional academic performance and productivity measures would be problematic for health law faculty members. The fact that they differ in the extent and/or nature of their research may mean that the criteria by which they are evaluated may need to be adjusted to reflect these differences. On the other hand, it may mean that these criteria have already been adjusted and the faculty members are responding to their program expectations.

Selecting a Health Care Law Teacher: Qualifications, Locating, Recruiting

The task force is persuaded that the core health law course should be taught by a lawyer, preferably one licensed to practice and with some professional experience. To the extent that developing a legal approach to problems that have legal implications is important for the student, the participation of the attorney is believed to be crucial.

Programs selecting full-time health care law teachers will be subject to the procedures mandated by the university. The program director, in addition to advertising in the usual sources for faculty, (for instance, *The Chronicle of Higher Education*, *The Nation's Health*, and *Staff Report on Education for Health Administration*), will want to network with other health care law teachers at health administration programs, the American Society of Law and Medicine and other health law organizations, law schools known for producing attorneys with an academic orientation, and other sources listed in Chapter 8. A review of recent publications in the area of health care law will generate the names of scholars working in the field.

The full-time health care law teacher should be chosen on the basis of his or her potential as a teacher, researcher, and colleague. For many programs, the concern will be (1) the range of courses to be offered by the teacher, (2) the teacher's relationships with other areas of the college or university (for example, the law school or department responsible for teaching business law), and (3) the chances that the individual will engage in a form of scholarly work that will eventually be recognized as suitable for merit, promotion, and tenure. Given the differences between legal research and the more traditional research carried out by Ph.D.s in health administration programs, it is important to have agreement at the time of initial employment among the candidate, the program, and the broader academic unit about the evaluation criteria to be used. The extensive outside commitments reported by the respondents to the survey signal a potential area of conflict between the attorney and those less likely and/or able to engage in consulting.

Adjunct faculty may be recruited from a variety of practitioner as well as academic pools. In reviewing the credentials of adjunct faculty having an active full-time practice, or of academics involved in programs and schools outside the health administration program, it is difficult to assess the extent to which a candidate is actually willing to make a commitment to a program, its students, and his own continuing education in those aspects of law most relevant to the program's students. Practitioner adjunct faculty may be found in a wide variety of settings, including solo and group law practice, health departments, and regulatory agencies. Adjunct academic faculty may be employed as members of the faculties of law schools and other health administration programs. Several survey respondents teach as adjunct faculty in more than one program.

The program director's role is to ensure that students are exposed to the materials and perspectives necessary for achieving the program's goals. The fact that health law teachers are often involved as practitioners in the day-to-day workings of the health care system may aid in the preparation of course materials relevant to the practice of health administration. On the other hand, the practitioner's view can become unbalanced, reflecting the peculiar focus of his own practice and clients.

The selection of a faculty member for a program should be based on past performance or promise for excellence in the classroom. Because of the unique nature of a program, the novice as well as the experienced teacher must be willing to take the time to design a course appropriate for the program. Given the investment in "start-up" time for this, the attorney's interest in a long-term relationship with the program is of great importance. It would also be hoped that the successful candidate would work with other faculty members to ensure that topics not covered in the health care law course are discussed elsewhere in the curriculum. In making a final selection the program director should give attention to the perceived willingness of the candidates to attend faculty meetings, engage in collaborative research with other faculty members, and work with the program at the time of accreditation.

It is important that the program director and faculty member assess the potential health care law teacher's knowledge and understanding of a broad range of medical/legal topics and come to some agreement on how the new teacher will gain the necessary knowledge to fulfill his or her role in the classroom. Continuing education and the use of outside guest speakers, discussed in other chapters, can be valuable here.

Retention of Adjunct Faculty

Retention of adjunct health care law teachers may be particularly difficult. Given the alternatives available for supplementing one's income, few attorneys assume adjunct faculty roles for this reason. At the same time, the demands made by programs may draw significantly on the health care law adjunct's time to the extent that his or her continued participation becomes difficult. There are a number of ways, however, that the demands made on the adjunct can be reduced, such as assistance in securing and distributing information, scheduling of meetings at times convenient for the adjunct, and financing of trips to professional meetings where the adjunct will be exposed to the broad range of materials necessary to teach a well-rounded course.

The Academic and Legal Cultures

The bulk of health law teachers have been trained in law schools that use teaching and research methods different from those methods found in non-law school environments. (A discussion of the appropriateness of these methods for teaching health administration students appears in Chapter 3.) Strong reliance on court cases and the Socratic method is often new to students in health administration programs. The difference has both positive and negative aspects: some students may be put off by it, while others may find it stimulating.

The law teacher's approach to his own work, the students, and the curriculum may appear to be "culturally" at odds with the approach taken by faculty members engaged in teaching such "hard" subjects as quantitative methods, finance, systems analysis, and computer methods. Even faculty in areas such as marketing and organizational behavior, which often use a case study teaching method, may find the lawyer's approach to case material quite different from the ways cases are designed to merge academics and practice in the classroom. These differences may not be important in themselves, but they can conspire to distance health law teachers from their faculty colleagues and, in subtle ways, make their full participation in the academic community more difficult.

Special Issues

The appropriate level of preparation for entry into courses is of concern throughout the health care administration curriculum. Once decisions have been made about the foundation courses desirable and required, program directors must make judgments concerning the extent to which a student's claim for waiver of a prerequisite or other requirement is met. The task force deliberations over these issues is reflected in the following discussion.

Prerequisites and business law.

In the vast majority of graduate and undergraduate programs, students enroll in one law course only. Programs may, however, insist that students fulfill some legal prerequisite to enrollment in the health care law course. The most common prerequisite discussed by the task force was a basic course in business law. Such a course may be required in undergraduate programs as part of the undergraduate business curriculum.

To meet the business law prerequisite of a master's-level program, the business law course may be taken prior to program entry or as a for-credit part of the graduate curriculum. Programs with a large proportion of business undergraduates will be most likely to have recruited students who have had a business law course.

If the one-course requirement prevails at the graduate and undergraduate levels, the depth of knowledge to be included in the course is an important issue. The task force members reached no consensus on this. It is the responsibility of program directors to familiarize themselves with the curriculum of the course and guide faculty members in the transmission of important information.

Exemptions. Graduate-level health administration students having trained in undergraduate health administration programs may ask for exemptions from the graduate legal requirement. It is not unusual to review requests for exemptions from students who completed courses that required the identical text as the required graduate course. Nevertheless, the task force believes that the goals and teaching methods of undergraduate and graduate courses are often sufficiently different that exemptions are warranted in only very unusual situations.

TOWARD A MANAGED CURRICULUM

We have argued that graduate programs in health services administration are engaged in focused/professional training and, at the undergraduate level, in general education within a framework of professional training. Those who doubt the diversity among courses and the variety of approaches for teaching will want to review the sample outlines in Chapter 9. Our review of the collected outlines revealed three broad "types" of courses: institutional management, public policy, and public health.

It was not always apparent that the focus identified for a specific course was correlated with the type of school in which the program was located (for example, business or public health). And within some of the larger universities in the United States, several health care law courses were offered, each meeting, to different degrees, the goals for educating a student wanting to enter a health services administration career.

To the extent that specific competencies and knowledge are identifiable for graduates of health services administration programs and that a boom in knowledge in health care law and specialization of lawyers has occurred, a managed curriculum, rather than a curriculum designed by an individual instructor, is appropriate. To achieve a managed curriculum, the program director must retain responsibility for knowing what is taught throughout the curriculum--by whom, and from what perspective. The health care attorney, well integrated into the program through the processes suggested above, is the key to achieving high-quality legal content in a managed curriculum. Both the program director and the attorney must recognize that health care law encompasses many issues requiring knowledge from broad areas of the law. The program director must actively question the adequacy of the legal component (both course and non-course work). In engineering the program's goals, the director must remember that "different lawyers know different things." The attorney who has specialized in malpractice may bring a very different focus to the classroom than a counterpart who has specialized, as an employee of the state, in the regulation of the nursing home industry. As the director raises questions relating to new areas of content, the attorney must act as adviser, suggesting where in the curriculum the materials might fit and the individual best suited for presenting the materials. It is only through a close working relationship between the program director and the health care law teacher that a strong managed curriculum can be achieved.

CHAPTER 3

TEACHING OBJECTIVES AND METHODS

Teaching is an art and a science. Successful teaching depends in large measure on mastery of effective skills and techniques by teachers. Although every teacher may intentionally or unintentionally, use his or her own "unique" methods, there are commonalities among both the problems that teachers face and the approaches that are utilized.

The survey results discussed later in this chapter reveal a remarkable consensus on the objectives of health law courses in health administration programs and the methods by which these courses are being taught. Nonetheless, for all of us in the field, these survey results should be used only as a starting point for analyzing the prospects for promoting more successful teaching.

It may help to differentiate among the numerous available teaching methods to remember Bloom's commonly used taxonomy of teaching objectives: knowledge, skills, attitudes. While all teaching intends to impart these elements in varying degrees, each particular choice of emphasis requires a different type of teaching style, mechanics, or method. For example, if knowledge is to be instilled, more individual student reading is indicated. If skill in articulating legal reasoning is the objective, student recitation might be encouraged. If attitudes are to be affected (for example, looking at all sides of an issue), class discussions or group projects might be valuable. It is too simplistic to divide teaching objectives into these three categories, but they remind us that objectives are multiple and should be defined for each teaching situation.

The challenge of teaching health law to students in health administration programs is successfully met only when attention is given to the characteristics of the environment in which health law courses are taught, the variety of objectives to be pursued, the assessment and selection of methods or tools with which to teach health law, and the evaluation of the accomplishment of course objectives.

Before one can design a health law course and select appropriate teaching objectives and methods, a number of factors must be identified and analyzed. We can call this process an "inventory assessment," which is an exercise that should be undertaken not just for each health administration program setting but periodically within each program. This includes a close look at both environment and objectives, as well as identification and study of teaching methods and evaluation techniques.

ENVIRONMENT

The inclusion of health law courses in a health administration curriculum at the graduate or undergraduate level may be accomplished in a variety of ways, depending on the goals of the particular program, the objectives and coverage of other courses, the availability of health law teachers and other resources, and the interest of faculty and students. Following are some environmental considerations in developing and offering health law in a health administration program.

Program Goals

As described in Chapter 2, it is important to coordinate program goals and course design. Program goals will dictate the amount of emphasis to be placed on law content in general and on different areas of health law. How much depth a given subject deserves is influenced by the intended career patterns of program graduates. Chapters 4 and 5 discuss the differences between graduate and undergraduate programs. If a program specializes in health planning or medical care organization or multisystem management, the selection of teaching objectives should take into account that emphasis and provide more depth in the related aspects of health law. If the program a more generic management emphasis, the law content objectives might be broader. Course design and implementation should address these different goals in terms of the knowledge, skills, and attitudes to be promoted in the program.

Course Setting

A significant constraint on selection of both objectives and methods for health law courses is the location of the course or courses in the curriculum. Very important is whether the program offers a single, freestanding course or a principal course followed by elective law courses or seminars. The number of contact hours permitted for the course, whether there are relevant prerequisites for the program (for example, business law), what courses precede and follow, whether the course is required or elective, and the number and types of other law-related courses offered are all factors that influence the design and teaching of a health law course. Just as it is important for the health law teacher to have a general familiarity with the objectives of other courses in the program curriculum, it is also good to know about the methods and techniques used by colleagues in their courses.

Physical Setting

Another aspect of course design is the physical space and support services available. It may be critical to determine the access to legal materials and other resources, such as law libraries, courtrooms, hospital counsel, practicing health lawyers, government agencies, and medicolegal or health law organizations. The possible participation of other lawyers on the university faculty or staff is also pertinent. Teaching space is limited in many health administration programs and may affect teaching decisions. For example, there are more teaching-method options in a multipurpose classroom than in a large amphitheater. Use of more than one site for the course may be required if special features are included, such as video recordings or mock trials. If a program furnishes audiovisual and video production services, computer equipment, full library services (including reserved books and videotapes), and small breakout or seminar rooms, then more imaginative approaches can be pursued. As described in Chapter 6, there are an increasing number and variety of teaching and demonstration aids and materials available, both commercially and through educational organizations. Selection of materials and techniques for teaching are, of course, limited by budget constraints; but careful planning and efficient use of resources (as in sharing the costs of a film with another group) will help.

Teachers

A course taught by a full-time, law-trained teacher may be different from one taught by part-time faculty or persons who are not law-trained or university-based. Our survey indicates that most health law teachers are lawyers. Also it has become apparent to us that a small but increasing number are full-time faculty members. Regardless of background, each teacher needs to assess his or her strengths and weaknesses as a teacher and develop ways to shore up those areas where improvement could be made. In some universities there are teaching laboratories where technical assistance is provided for developing or polishing teaching skills. Other opportunities for self-improvement may exist within a program or through involvement with national organizations. For example, AUPHA has sponsored various workshops on teaching methods, and the American Society of Law and Medicine sponsors an annual Health Law Teachers Conference in which both teaching materials and methods are presented.

Students

Earlier discussion focused on differences in student goals. There is also great diversity in background and experience of students, both among and within programs. The age and previous work experience in the health field of students has a bearing on how a course may be structured and taught. The class profile will vary from year to year, requiring an annual assessment.

The sophistication of the students creates opportunities for and limitations on the selection of approach and methods. For example, the level of discussion around a case study in each group of students will vary markedly depending on the personal familiarity of students with technical terminology and case context. In dissecting and debating *Canterbury v. Spence*, a landmark case, for instance, a former nurse might be more fluent about consent to treatment options than a younger student who has not been in a hospital since birth.

This diversity raises the problem for teachers of determining an equitable approach in conducting the course. It is neither necessary nor feasible to expect equality of experience among students, but it is desirable to fix a minimum baseline level of knowledge. Here the familiar dilemma must be faced about how many of the students should be expected to learn how much of the material. In other words, should the teacher adjust the course pace and complexity so that 50 percent of the students understand 100 percent of the material? Or should the course be simplified so that 90 percent of the students understand 100 percent of the material? There may be some portion of the course content that all students should learn, such as basic legal definitions. But perhaps it is acceptable for only 10 percent of the students to master legal reasoning--for instance, understand the complex antitrust case of *Hyde v. Jefferson* well enough to analyze the implications of various vertical integration options in a joint venture between a hospital and a nursing home in specific market settings. It may be easier for the lawyer-teacher to pretend that the health administration students are all third-year law students and give them fast-paced, erudite lectures, but that approach may not meet the goals of the program. Just as obvious, any attempt to dilute health law to a level of universal comprehension would be an insult to the average health administration student, as well as unjustifiably inefficient. The particular student group must be assessed and objectives adjusted before optimum teaching to occur.

Uniqueness of Law

As pointed out in earlier chapters, the field of law differs from the other disciplines in the health administration curriculum, such as quantitative methods, accounting and finance, organizational behavior, decision sciences, human resources management, and economics. It is not as concrete as accounting or as theoretical as organizational behavior. Law is a verbal field, debate oriented and analytic, containing its own substance and rules but applying to common experience. Law is a subject about which everyone knows something and most have misconceptions. Legislation, regulations, and court rulings are important parts of the field of health administration and the work of administrators, yet not subjects that nonlawyers can master. Law pervades nearly every course in a health administration curriculum, but legal process and principles cannot be adequately understood in those differing contexts without special preparation in legal fundamentals.

Students are attracted by the law's application in everyday life, its pervasiveness in health care management, and its pivotal role in health policy decision making. A course in health law might provide answers to questions that have arisen in other courses or contexts. It offers a chance to learn about how a lawyer thinks, perhaps to pierce the professional mystique. Additionally, a health law course may be seen as a refreshing respite from the rigidity of "number-crunching" courses.

For all these reasons and more, health law is different from other fields in a health administration program curriculum. Its uniqueness can be viewed as an advantage for a health law teacher in terms of course differentiation, substantive freshness, and inherent student interest. As a special subject in the curriculum, it provides the teacher with a positive base upon which to build a course. But the distinctiveness of law as a professional field makes it difficult to integrate into the curriculum and to coordinate with overall health administration program objectives.

Accreditation Standards

In analyzing the environmental factors that affect the teaching of health law, it is important to determine the criteria that may be applied for purposes of accreditation. The Accrediting Commission on Education for Health Services Administration (ACEHSA) requires that health administration curricula include health law content. For an individual program, ACEHSA will examine the appropriateness of the health law content relative to program goals. A separate course in health law is not necessarily expected, although many programs have chosen to satisfy the content requirement by offering one or more courses. It is important to observe that there are no published or formal guidelines for either content or methods pertaining to health law teaching. Accreditation standards encourage program development of knowledge and skills that well-designed health law courses and research projects can help achieve. In fulfilling accreditation objectives both program directors and health law teachers keep abreast of health law activities in other health administration programs and in the field in general.

OBJECTIVES

The task force's survey indicates that the objectives pursued by health law teachers in their courses vary considerably among health administration programs (see Table 3-1). However, three major categories predominate: general legal principles, liability issues, and specific practical application of the law to health administration.

A sampling of course outlines obtained through the survey reveals both similarities and significant differences in stated course objectives. Below are some statements from those outlines. They are presented here not as models

TABLE 3-1 Objectives of Health Law Teachers (Survey Results)

Objective	Included (percent)
General legal principles	95
Liability issues	93
Specific practical applications	85
How to work with lawyers	71
Legal reasoning process	68
Dealing with government agencies	51
Health policy	39
Other	7

or as complete descriptions of the objectives that the courses seek to achieve, but rather as representations of the attempts by health law teachers to express the objectives of a particular course in a specific health administration program and its setting. Notice both the similarities and differences in course titles and the phrasing of objectives, suggesting that courses are designed to achieve individual results in a common field. Within a program there may also be additional law-related courses that pursue other, complementary objectives.

Schools of Public Health

"To make students aware of legal issues relating to the management and administration of a health care institution and the role of professional management." (Legal Aspects of Hospital and Health Care Administration, University of Michigan)

"To provide students with the opportunity to master basic legal principles and concepts, develop the ability to recognize legal issues and make the best use of the legal personnel they will have access to in their professional capacities." (Health and Hospital Law, University of Pittsburgh)

"Introduction to the area of public policy and its relationship to legislation in the health field. Basic knowledge will be established concerning fundamental concepts of law and legislation, the legislative process, and formal and informal influences which shape the final enactment of significant legislation." (Legislation and Organization for Health and Social Services, University of California, Berkeley)

"To provide a general background for understanding the judicial and administrative systems and the effect of federal/state jurisdictional problems and the separation of powers issues in the context of the health care delivery system." (Public Health Law, San Diego State University)

Medical Schools

"To acquaint health administration students with current and future legal and policy issues in the health care field, through an examination of laws, regulations, court decisions and the legal process; to develop skills in understanding legal terminology, identifying legal issues and determining when to obtain legal assistance; and to demonstrate the relevance of law in solving management problems and making health policy decisions, both in theory and in practice." (Law in Health Administration, Duke University)

"To familiarize the student with principles and rules of law in general and how these rules apply to health administration." (Health Law, Washington University)

Business Schools

"Students will examine a number of legal problems so that they will become acquainted with the basic legal principles and their application to the health care system and be able to recognize legal issues inherent in health care administration and become familiar with legal literature." (Health Care Jurisprudence, Arizona State University)

"A historical and current overview of legal regulation of the health care enterprise. By following developments from the past to the present, it is possible to gain insight into what will likely come about in the future. Of particular interest are the social, ethical, and public policy issues the law addresses in trying to balance the rights of individuals against the needs and concerns of a modern society." (Legal Aspects of Health Care, The Wharton School, University of Pennsylvania)

Undergraduate Programs

"To provide the health care administration student with a framework for the understanding of the legal climate within which the health care institution operates. Emphasis is placed upon those legal concepts which bear most heavily upon the operation, planning, and decision-making activities of the health care administrator." (Health Care Legal Aspects, Xavier University)

"To demonstrate judicial interaction with hospital and health care problems, the focus being on private rather than public law. Convey enough knowledge of the law so that the student will be able to recognize legal issues arising in situations likely to be encountered in his ultimate position as a health care administrator." (Legal Aspects of Health Care Administration, Trinity University)

Strategic Considerations

Consultation or comparison with health law courses in other health administration programs is obviously beneficial, but it would be neither appropriate nor prudent to replicate these courses.

Determining the objectives of a health law course, or series of courses, in a health administration program is necessarily a complex task and should not be done in isolation from the rest of the health administration curriculum. A common problem in health administration programs is duplication in introducing some generic information to students. For example, the third-party reimbursement system may be important for law courses as well as finance and policy courses, but the basics need not be covered in both courses. Nevertheless, some overlap among courses may be appropriate, if deliberately planned. Course effectiveness will depend as much on careful planning and design as on the classroom skills and techniques of the teacher.

In summary, health law course objectives should be specifically and individually developed with full respect given to the factors that will enable the course to be taught as an integrated, coordinated, and complementary part of the overall health administration program. It should be recalled that the chosen objectives for health law courses are a function of the array of environmental considerations discussed earlier.

METHODS

Course Management

A commitment to the discipline of teaching requires the development of "course management" skills. To ensure a successful learning experience for students, an instructor must adhere to course design, be prepared, furnish expected materials, meet class and office hours, effectively manage the available time in a class period, control classroom activities, ensure the availability of assistance outside of class, and comply with program grading and evaluation policies.

Part-Time Faculty Members

While not all program faculty expectations may apply to part-time teachers, the effective management of a course is just as critical for part-time as full-time faculty.

Both face the same challenges of motivation and pursuit of course objectives. Both must select the best methods for achieving those objectives. In the case of adjunct teachers, however, it becomes doubly important to give careful attention to course management, since availability outside of class may be limited. Time management is also crucial, especially when a large block of time (say, two to three hours) is allotted for a weekly class. Effective planning may include a clock next to lecture notes and methodical setting of specific objectives for each session. As discussed in Chapter 2, the program director has a responsibility to enable part-time teachers to make the most effective use of program facilities and resources.

Teaching Methods

Survey data show that a variety of methods and techniques are being used in teaching health law (Table 3-2). It is apparent that no single approach to teaching has become the exclusive format in this field, although the survey indicates that lecture coupled with class discussion clearly is the most popular format.

TABLE 3-2 Methods for Teaching Health Law (Survey Results)

Method	Used (percent)
Lecture plus Q&A	88
Student presentations	46
Guest lecture (1-3 times/semester)	37
Lecture mainly	17
Guest lecture (4+ times/semester)	15
Team teaching	12
Other	7

The survey data may camouflage a wider variety of teaching formats than is indicated. For example, "lecture plus Q&A" may have been marked by teachers who use a true law school type of Socratic method, stating a case or problem and eliciting viewpoints from the class, as well as by those who simply give a straight lecture and invite questions at the end. In between are a variety of methods, such as case discussions of the business school type where class members present various facets of the case based on changing assumptions.

More revealing from the survey is the variety of teaching techniques used by health law teachers (Table 3-3). Here too a wide range of devices is used, with the so-called Socratic dialogue and legal research project assignments being popular among most teachers.

TABLE 3-3 Teaching Techniques Used by Health Law Teachers (Survey Results)

Technique	Used (percent)
Socratic dialogue	68
Legal research project	56
Law library tour	32
Audiovisual aids	32
Role playing	22
Mock trials	22
Students assist in research	12
Visits to courts or agencies	10
Students assist consulting	5
Other	7

A note about using law school teaching techniques

If one of the course objectives is to familiarize students with legal reasoning or to make them appreciate the thinking process of lawyers, then some degree of exposure to customary law school teaching techniques, using various forms of the Socratic method, is beneficial. These techniques, as applied to health law courses, clearly may take more forms than the stereotypical style of interrogation and intimidation of students by a dominating teacher. In fact, some might argue that the classic Socratic style is inappropriate for teaching non-law students. The hard-edged, challenging teaching tactics that are employed in law classes to create an adversarial attitude must be used with caution. Without the milieu of a full law school curriculum, some typical law school teaching techniques will not only miss the mark, but possibly cause misconceptions about law and lawyers. Nevertheless, selective exposure of students to the flavor of law school teaching may be beneficial and constructive in the context of a health law course.

In order to understand the interplay among teaching methods and techniques, classroom formats and mechanisms, and teacher styles and preferences, it may be helpful to examine some of the options more fully.

Lectures

Some health law teachers are skilled orators who can use organizational techniques, oral skills, and selected presentation devices to deliver a balanced and effective package of information. Most of us are more limited in our experience, ability, and natural stage presence. Effective front-of-the-room lectures are very difficult to deliver on a consistent basis. The abundance of substantive health law, however, invites consideration of this method for advancing some concepts and principles, such as the background and application of antitrust law. A lecture or two might be the quickest means of introducing the Anglo-American judicial system to a nonlawyer, especially if the lectures are coupled with appropriate reading assignments.

Avoidance of classroom discussion and limiting questions from students will allow the instructor to control both the teaching time and unnecessary diversions. Especially for large classes or those with a wide diversity of students, the lecture-only method is the most efficient and can be very effective. Nevertheless, there are limitations both in terms of objectives to be achieved (such as the legal reasoning process or sharpening of debating skills) and student interest span (including associated naivete about law) that weigh against the heavy use of the lecture-only method in most settings. Furthermore, this method denies the teacher the feedback needed to tailor the course to the class.

Lectures plus discussions

The most popular teaching method is the lecture coupled or interspersed with class discussion. This is the style of teaching most health law teachers were weaned on, so it follows that this would be the model with which they are most comfortable. However, this format as used in health law classes around the country no doubt includes a wide range of techniques, depending on what approach is appropriate for the subject matter and what a teacher has become experienced in doing. For example, a class on "authorization for treatment" might take the form of a chalkboard or slide-assisted lecture outlining the principles of assault and battery, and negligence and privacy followed by student questions (and perhaps student answers) based on their readings. One professor reported that he begins his classes on this topic by lightly touching the shoulder of a student on the front row, asking students to decide whether it was a tort, and then posing a series of more substantial touchings, finally raising the specter of medical experimentation on unconscious and unknowing patients. Another professor relates the interesting fact situation in *Canterbury v. Spence* and promotes students to discuss various rationales the court might have used in deciding this case. A further variation might be the drawing out of the principles of informed consent by a Socratic questioning of one or more students, leading finally to an acceptable consensus of understanding. Still another method is a videotape about consent used in combination with the teacher's chalkboard summation of the principles based on student responses.

Case method

Closely related to the above discussion of the Socratic method is the issue of when and how to use the case method. First of all, for most health law teachers, the case method means law school style rather than business school style. In other courses in a health administration curriculum, the student likely will have become accustomed to case discussions of the business school type. While there may be differences in both objectives and techniques in conducting the two case discussion methods, the most obvious distinction is the use of reported court decisions in law schools and the use of real or simulated stories of business situations or corporate histories in business schools. If done well, both types of case discussion methods can stir keen interest and simulation of real-life problem solving.

The health law teacher may find that students relish the chance to read actual court decisions, only to find themselves lost in the procedural issues that permeate most cases. Some of this confusion can be avoided by using edited case materials. The other major obstacle in using court cases is the relative inefficiency of teaching principles and process when a large number of cases are required to demonstrate the desired points. Students may balk at the amount of advance reading, followed by sometimes cursory or perfunctory treatment of certain cases in class. Some material, such as regulatory issues, may not be as interesting in case form. Ambitious teachers may construct composite cases to demonstrate a variety of points more efficiently, but that is a time-consuming task.

One solution to the problem of putting cases into context is the use of law review articles that give brief but critical attention to numerous cases while presenting historical development and legal analysis in language most health administration students can comprehend. Many teachers have found that law reviews are a rich source of material for both reading assignments and research projects. The format of law review articles is particularly suited to teaching, since it is a balance of background detail, legal reasoning, and careful speculation about legal issues. Some might even say that a well-written law review piece is the culmination of a lawyer's skill.

Teaching by using cases puts a much greater burden on the teacher to develop the context and fill in the interstices. Even so, students may begin to sense that they are learning only discrete, disjointed concepts, not a comprehensive body of knowledge. If the course objective were only to appreciate legal reasoning and understand some scattered substantive health law, then a case course would be appropriate. But with the general assumption in health administration programs that more should be taught in a health law course, it is necessary to mix the case method with other teaching techniques.

Legal research projects and student presentations

Expectations about non-law students doing sophisticated legal research and making stimulating in-class presentations on legal topics must be adjusted to account for the amount of exposure to legal research that health administration students receive. There is value in conducting the exercise, since even minimal experience in pursuit of legal research can be a rewarding revelation about the complexity of legal analysis. In this connection conducted tours of the law library may be required for students to be able to accomplish even simple legal research assignments. The law library staff members will probably be willing to assist in such tours (if only to protect themselves from later ad hoc requests for orientation). Doing research in the law library provides some rubbing of shoulders with law students, perhaps aiding in the objective of learning how to relate to lawyers.

Even more valuable to students are health law research projects that require the student to consult with the hospital counsel or a practicing health lawyer about some aspect of the project. The teacher can sometimes arrange this to be of mutual benefit, with the student being assigned a real-life problem and sharing the research results with the outside lawyer. While such practical research assignments may be problematic, there is the possibility of a lasting learning experience if successful. At the other end of the spectrum, but still of value, an assignment based simply on designated law journal articles will give the health administration student a new perspective about legal research.

The impact of a student paper or oral presentation on a health law topic can be enhanced in at least three ways:

1. Ensure that a limited, researchable health law topic is chosen--contained in scope and predictable in result--so that the student has a chance to be both accurate and satisfied with a positive experience. For example, assigning "Can AIDS patients be quarantined?" is more appropriate than "What are the legal aspects of AIDS?"

2. Provide teacher assistance (including loaning books and articles) to the student to ensure a more effective and reliable paper, so that the student is not misled by his or her own legal conclusions and, in the case of an oral presentation, fellow students are not misled. For example, if the issue is whether a hospital can insulate itself from emergency room liability by careful wording of its contract with a group of emergency room physicians, then the teacher should consult with the student about current case law and legislation affecting the matter, and for the purpose of reality, perhaps provide a sample contract for the student to critique.

3. Evaluate the performance of each student's paper or presentation. Even though this may consume a considerable amount of time and effort, it is necessary to ensure that the event is a positive learning experience for the student and not merely a reinforcement of bad habits. If the student has submitted a paper that is replete with errors in grammar and spelling, it might be returned to him or her for correction before being resubmitted for content evaluation.

Videotaping of student presentations can reinforce the seriousness of preparation and presentation, as well as provide an effective evaluation tool for both individual and peer study.

Guest lectures

The use of outside or adjunct faculty, such as practicing attorneys (both plaintiff's bar and defense bar), insurance professionals from industry or government, labor relations consultants, hospital counsel, and other professionals can be effective if the guests are carefully instructed as to their role in the course. The danger here is that speakers may be engaged who are informative or entertaining but who do not necessarily fit into the course progression or plan.

Perhaps the most ineffective type of course design is the exclusive use of guest speakers; there is little likelihood that the students' learning objectives will be satisfied, regardless of how distinguished the speakers. Continuity and consistency are usually lost, while redundancy and gaps in coverage are often the result. If other university faculty are used, there may be a better chance of course objectives being achieved, but again, advance preparation of any guest lecturer is required for a satisfactory use of teaching time. Some teachers have found it useful to intersperse regular lectures with guest lectures on specific topics. Also, teachers may effectively interact with visiting experts to the benefit of the students. A new teacher may find more need for guest lecturers in his or her initial teaching and substitute his or her own presentations in later semesters.

Team teaching

Joining with other faculty members to design and conduct a health law course can be both frustrating and exhilarating. Team teaching can produce dynamics in the classroom that reward the extra efforts of preparation. Care must be taken to maintain continuity and coordination. If both (or all) instructors attend every class session, better coordination is achieved. One special advantage for health law courses using two lawyers is the nearly inevitable display of differing legal points of view. If faculty members from other fields are joined in the course, the advantage is the comparison of law with other disciplines and the possible integration of different approaches to a given problem.

Role playing and mock trials

Any attempt to move students out of the role of observers or passive learners into that of active participants in a simulated legal transaction or judicial process will pay off. Role playing using scripts or an ad lib style can be an effective exposure to different perspectives.

For example, acting as a hospital trustee debating the pros and cons of changing from a nonprofit corporation to a for-profit enterprise is a lively way to discover more about corporation and tax law. A simulated encounter between an errant physician being suspended from the medical staff and his or her attorney could be a productive way to examine the issue of credentialing. Reading the cross-examination of the administration's witnesses in *Darling v. Charleston Memorial Hospital*, a landmark hospital liability case, or a more recent corporate liability case is a memorable way to achieve both knowledge and attitude objectives. If a discussion ensues about what makes an effective expert witness in a court trial or an administrative hearing, then new skills may also be imparted.

The more attention given to preparation of scripts, practice by participants, and conducive physical setting, the better the results. Most students have a natural bent for acting out assigned roles and seem to rise to the challenge of making it a positive learning experience.

Using students as research assistants

The use by an instructor of students for research, or even consulting activities (if permitted by university policies), can be a genuinely educational experience for a student. It may, however, be a time-consuming exercise for the instructor in providing sufficient supervision of the project and review of the products. The special difficulty in health administration programs is the selection of students who are capable of performing reliable research on health law topics. To the extent that such students can be assigned tasks that are elementary enough to be accomplished yet complex enough for academic growth, the use of student assistants can be considered a unique technique for teaching health law. For example, a student who locates and copies cases or articles, or who proofreads a manuscript, or who designs a survey instrument may well consider the experience educational. Nevertheless, this practice cannot substitute for participation in well-designed health law courses and should only be considered as an enhancement opportunity for students especially interested in health law. The teacher must be willing to commit the time and have specific teaching objectives in mind when students do research projects.

Other methods and techniques

The survey did not disclose much use of other teaching tools or approaches by health law teachers. It could be expected, however, that considerable experimentation takes place in classrooms of both new and experienced teachers. The eventual incorporation of novel methods and techniques should depend on a close scrutiny of their effectiveness in achieving course objectives. Consultation with colleagues both in health law and other disciplines would be beneficial. One of the advantages of teaching in a health administration program is the mixture of teachers and teaching methods used in the diverse courses that make up a typical curriculum. Health law teachers should welcome the advice and suggestions of colleagues.

In addition there is a considerable body of literature on teaching methods. One of the most popular sources is Wilbur J. McKeachie's *Teaching Tips: A Guidebook for the Beginning College Teacher*, now in its seventh edition (1978). The book discusses the theories and practices of teaching and includes a checklist of teaching techniques and goals potentially achieved. The following techniques are listed: books, lectures, discussions, PSI (personalized system of instruction), student panels and reports, guest lecturers or resource persons, films and videotapes, slides, bulletin boards and mock-ups, recordings, field trips, laboratories, role playing, buzz groups, study guides and workbooks, periodicals, teaching machines and programmed texts, and computer-aided instruction. McKeachie also presents a special section on instructional games, simulations, and the case method. A health law teacher would of course need to adapt some of the discipline-specific methods to health law.

EVALUATION

The evaluation process is dependent on health administration program and university policies as well as on the instructor's capacity to devise effective methods. It is widely agreed that law school essay-type examinations are not the most efficient or effective way to evaluate the performance of non-law students. Other methods in use in health law courses include modified essay-type exams (using health administration or health law situations or questions), objective tests (multiple choice, true/false, matching, short answer, and so on), research papers (on a class-wide or individual topic), oral presentations (in class or staged before video cameras), take-home problems (such as in basket exercises, open book examinations, or overnight research memoranda), and combinations of these.

The type of evaluation method used should be selected with the course objectives in mind. The following chart demonstrates the types of considerations that might be applied in devising an evaluation method.

Objective	Evaluation
Legal reasoning, identification of legal issues, thinking like a lawyer, use of legal terminology	Law school essay questions, legal research papers, take-home problems
Legal concepts and principles	Essay questions, short-answer questions
Legal definitions, selected points of law	Short-answer questions, multiple choice, true/false
Application of law in health administration	Constructed case problems, legal research papers
Communication with lawyers	Legal research papers, oral presentations, role playing, mock trials

Although this chart is only exemplary, each health law teacher can follow a similar process in determining the most effective evaluation tools for specific courses.

Other evaluation techniques may be borrowed from other fields. For example, in continuing education, considerable use is made of pre-tests and post-tests to measure learning success. And there are various individualized evaluation devices, such as fulfillment of learning contracts and special criteria for mastery of learning.

The most common form of evaluation in current educational practice is the course examination in either essay or multiple-choice format. Educational literature offers numerous rules for constructing essay tests, including the following:

    1.   Provide clear and unambiguous directions.

2. Measure only complex learning outcomes requiring the synthesis or evaluation of ideas.

3. Design each question for specific outcomes, not inviting "fishing expeditions."

4. Allow ample time, preferably stated, for each question.

There are also rules for scoring essay examinations:

1. Measure only learning outcomes. Other factors, such as gratuitous information, spelling, grammar, or style are irrelevant unless expressly stated in the learning objectives.
2. A unit point method is desirable and should be based on a model answer.

3. Evaluate all students' answers to one question before moving on to the next question.

4. Mask the students' identities during evaluation.

5. Use a second evaluator when possible.

When multiple-choice tests are used, most of the teacher's work is in the careful design and construction of a fair and useful instrument. Here are some rules of construction:

1. Make each item connected to a specific learning objective.

2. Present a single, clearly formulated problem in the stem.

3. Most of the wording should be in the stem.

4. Positive wording is clearer than negative wording.

5. The intended answer should be clearly the best.

6. Use consistent grammar in all alternative answers.

7. Avoid verbal clues and positioner length clues.

8. Make alternative distractor answers plausible and attractive to the uninformed.

9. Avoid use of "all of the above."

Scoring multiple-choice tests should take account of weights the teacher may choose to assign to different aspects of the evaluation. One effective method for improving an examination vehicle is to analyze the wrong or inappropriate answers.

GRADING

The assignment of grades must conform with program and university rules, but each teacher has considerable discretion under any system in establishing or applying criteria. Again the purpose of grading should be recognized, since it may fulfill diverse functions. Grades are ordinarily used to determine a student's status in the program but may be used as information for the student's self-improvement, as data for promotion and tenure decisions, or for education research projects.

Regardless of the grading system or its purposes, there are special problems that face health law teachers in assigning grades. The mixture of students with different backgrounds and preparation may present problems of equitable assignment, raising the issue of achievement versus effort. Also perplexing is the transference of grades from the health law class back to other units or schools, raising questions of definitions and equivalence. Overriding these technical concerns is the frustration of attempting to introduce the complex discipline of law to non-law students and then having to grade these students who have not had the time or the opportunity to master more than the rudimentary levels of the subject.

Ultimately, each health law teacher must arrive at an acceptable definition of proficiency in health law in order to apply grades to students in health administration programs on a fair and equitable basis.

CONCLUSION

This discussion of teaching objectives, methods, and evaluation concepts is presented with full knowledge that experienced teachers have developed widely differing approaches. Each may have found effectiveness in particular ways and for varying lengths of time. Most successful teachers have kept their minds open to new ideas and techniques. They have had the confidence to experiment with different methods and have kept up with what other successful teachers are doing. In the end, each teacher must put together that combination of skills and concepts that works best for him or her. It is important to remember that as time passes, conditions change and so too must each teacher's approach to teaching. Effective teaching requires a constant process of renewal and revision.

CHAPTER 4

CONTENT OF GRADUATE HEALTH LAW COURSES

The Health Law Teachers Survey requested faculty of AUPHA member programs to state the purposes and objectives of their health law course(s), submit course outlines and reading lists, and rank the relative "importance to students" of each subject matter area contained on a detailed list of possible/probable course contents. This chapter reviews the findings of the survey and makes recommendations on subject matter content of graduate-level health law courses.

The content of a course or courses in health law will be influenced and, in fact, determined by an array of factors. Since health law cannot be fairly characterized as a functional field of law *per se*--akin to contracts, torts, or the law of property--the teacher must exercise great care in selecting topics for study in light of the factors most relevant to the program in which the course is taught. Virtually all substantive and procedural subject matter areas of the law--an entire three-year law school curriculum and more--have an impact on the delivery and financing of health care. The task is to select carefully those topics most relevant to the objectives of the course, the career goals of the students, the maturity and academic level of the students, and the educational mission of the program in which the course or courses are taught. Secondary factors influencing course content will be academic prerequisites to the study of health law, availability of other cognate courses taught by faculty colleagues, and contact teaching hours available.

SETTINGS

Programs at the master's degree level are labeled with a variety of titles and are situated in a diversity of schools within the university community. Titles include health care administration, health planning, health services management, health policy, and medical care organization, as well as a combination of these terms. Schools supporting the program in particular university settings and awarding the degrees include business administration, management, public health, medicine, public administration, and community and allied health. In similar fashion, the particular degree awarded differs in terminology: Master of Business Administration, Master of Health Services Administration, Master of Public Health, and Master of Public Administration, for example.

Since the programs differ so much from university to university on the bases of the sponsoring school, the nature of the curriculum, and the emphasis of the program, the credentials of faculty may also differ. In turn, the academic objectives of the program and the career aspirations of the graduates vary from university to university. In planning courses in health law, the faculty member must act in concert with the school's and program's educational objectives and keep ever mindful of the students' professional career plans. An individual's contemplated career certainly has a direct bearing on his or her need for particular knowledge and skills. This reality is true for law as well as for the other disciplines typically taught in a graduate program in health administration.

There are currently more than 90 graduate programs at the master's degree level in the United States and Canada. Of these, 50 are full members of the Association of University Programs in Health Administration and accredited by the Accrediting Commission on Education for Health Services Administration (ACEHSA). ACEHSA was specifically created as an accrediting agency for academic programs in health administration. It is cosponsored by a number of different professional organizations, including the American College of Health Care Administrators, American College of Healthcare Executives, American College of Medical Group Administrators, American Health Planning Association, American Hospital Association, Association of Mental Health Administrators, and Association of University Programs in Health Administration.

In addition, many of the schools in which health administration programs are situated are programmatically accredited in their respective professional fields. Schools of business administration, for example, are accredited by the American Assembly of Collegiate Schools of Business and schools of public health by the Council for Education in Public Health. Some of the graduate programs in health care administration offer joint or dual degrees in cooperation with their university's graduate school of business administration and/or law school. Thus, for instance, some universities encourage a student to gain both a Master of Health Sciences Administration and a Master of Business Administration. Typically, such a dual-degree program in administration can be completed in three academic years. Since the legal aspects of health care have become so pervasive, a few universities have developed dual degrees in health administration and law, typically requiring a four-year program of study. All these factors regarding the school or discipline that sponsors the program in health administration, the development of joint and dual degrees, and the educational objectives of a particular program will influence the content of health law courses.

Career Goals

The content of courses in health law should be determined in part by the stated educational goals of the degree program in which the course(s) is offered and the educational/career track of the students. A course in law or legal medicine taught in medical school, for example, would likely contain various subjects that would not be covered at all, or would be mentioned only briefly, in a course designed for students preparing for administrative careers in the health care industry. Moreover, both subject matter content and depth of coverage (as distinct from breadth) will be influenced by whether the course is a graduate or undergraduate offering.

It is submitted that graduate students preparing for mid-management positions in large, complex health care organizations or who anticipate entering the field by initially accepting a residency in administration (some degree programs require all graduates to complete an administrative residency) or a fellowship working closely with a senior executive (a preceptor) are in need of a somewhat different academic exposure to the legal aspects of health care administration than undergraduate students. First, they need significant practice in analytic skills and critical thinking. The appropriate selection of course content and study materials can cultivate these skills. Second, since these students will generally be working more closely with senior management, it is advisable that they be provided an opportunity for in-depth exposure to legal issues that relate directly and specifically to both patient care issues and the development of longer-range institutional policies. Thus, graduate students can benefit from case discussions of physician malpractice and expected standards of care; corporate responsibility for monitoring standards of practice; risk management; quality assurance; hospital-physician relationships; termination of treatment for the hopelessly ill; corporate reorganization; nonprofit status; efforts to diversify an institution's activities; government regulatory and reimbursement mechanisms; and antitrust litigation. These matters and others require the attention of mid-level and senior management. Moreover, they require the development, implementation, and constant review of institutional day-to-day managerial policy.

In short, the graduate student preparing for a career in institutional management needs a broader, yet more specialized, approach to hospital-health law than the undergraduate. To put the matter another way, the specific applicability of tort, contract, and corporate law to the mission of the health care institution must be studied. While this is being done, many of the detailed substantive rules of contract (or tort) law taught in the traditional business law course will necessarily be largely ignored. For example, a business law course in contracts will typically teach the details of offer and acceptance, the capacity to contract, the doctrine of consideration, and the remedies available to the aggrieved party upon the nonperformance of a contractual obligation. In a course on hospital or health law, there will not be time for both business law fundamentals and health care applications. A business law course should not double as a hospital or health law course.

PROGRAM OUTCOMES

Despite the diversity in sponsorship and the varying titles of degrees awarded, the goals and educational objectives of the various health administration programs can be categorized and summarized as follows.

Three identifiable goals emerge from a reading of each program's educational objectives, as gathered through the task force's survey of health law teachers. The first and predominant goal is to provide training for administrators in the organization and management of entities in the health care industry. The second is to prepare students for positions of responsibility in health planning or management consulting, as distinct from institutional management. And the third is to emphasize educational courses and experiences that stress research and the formulation of public policy relative to access, availability, and financing of health care. These goals and objectives are formulated to coincide with employment opportunities and career plans for graduates. Some universities provide training for all four career opportunities--institutional management, planning, management consulting, and policy-making--by making various curriculum tracks or options available to the student. Inevitably, however, on many campuses, a single goal--and hence career track--will be emphasized and predominate as a result of limited economic and human resources.

Educational training for day-to-day institutional management is clearly the primary objective of most master's degree programs. In a broader, more general context, the Commission on Education for Health Administration (1975) has defined the process of administration as follows:

> Health Administration is planning, organizing, directing, controlling, coordinating, and evalu-

ating the resources and procedures by which needs and demands for health and medical care and a healthful environment are fulfilled by the provision of specific services to individual clients, organizations, and communities.[1]

Some degree programs emphasize that they seek graduate students capable of eventually assuming senior management responsibility in large, complex multihospital or health care systems. Others stress training for executive positions in entities providing out-of-hospital personal health services, such as nursing homes and other types of facilities for long-term care, ambulatory care, clinics, group medical practices, rural health care clinics, emergency medical care facilities, and the administration of mental health services. Some programs encourage each student to concentrate in a particular functional area: finance, marketing, quantitative methods, organizational behavior, or industrial relations. A few draw academic distinctions between administration of public or government institutions and private enterprise. In any event, the graduate schools commonly state that they focus on preparing individuals for analytic, critical problem solving and decision making and that most courses of instruction will develop skills and concepts rather than be merely descriptive of subject matter. Not infrequently, the schools claim that their graduates will someday be in "leadership" or "top management" positions, even that of the chief executive officer of a complex multi-institutional health care system. It is certainly true that today's senior health care administrators face an increasing array of difficult problems requiring imaginative and innovative problem-solving abilities. An aging population, continually escalating costs of care, limited resources, technological advances, and increasing government involvement in health care all combine to complicate the work of an administrator in the health care industry.

Courses in health law are ideal vehicles to encourage logical analysis and critical thinking. The Socratic method of teaching law should not be abandoned or considered dead and buried. After all, the very essence of law is to resolve conflicts of interest, settle disputes, and solve problems. This is not to say that law comes into play and that lawyers get involved only after actual litigation or a serious adversarial relationship arises. The law provides guidance in advance of litigation for the solving of problems and the avoidance of disputes. When structured and taught in an analytic framework, together with the appropriate use of appellate court cases and law review commentaries, health law courses can make a substantial contribution to the educational goals stated by the graduate schools. Lawyers can readily contribute to developing and enhancing the problem-solving capabilities of their students simply because the study of law involves the weighing and balancing of all relevant interests in a given complicated set of facts.

The second identifiable educational purpose of graduate programs in health administration is to prepare students for positions of responsibility in health planning or consulting, as distinct from day-to-day institutional management. These persons are typically employed by area-wide planning agencies, government regulatory agencies, private consulting firms, large hospitals, and multi-institutional providers of care. An increasing number of institutional providers, especially multi-institutional health care systems, have determined that it is desirable--indeed necessary--to have a full-time corporate/strategic planning department. All indications are that health planning will continue to develop and be recognized as a discipline of its own. Accordingly, many educational institutions have developed specialized curricula in this discipline and have encouraged faculty to conduct research in the area.

What is health planning? A generic definition is provided by Steven Sieverts, Vice-President for Institutional Affairs and Health Care Cost Containment, Blue Cross and Blue Shield of Greater New York. Mr. Sieverts defines planning as an activity that leads up to decision making. As such, it must be seen as essentially a thinking process, a gathering of facts, a testing of assumptions, a forecasting of the future, and a weighing of alternatives.[2]

Thus, in Mr. Sieverts' view, planning is more than a government activity regulating private decision making. Although regulatory planning is clearly a feature of the health care industry, the broader, generic concept of a planning responsibility reveals that the tasks justify full-time activity. Day-to-day managers simply do not have the time--and sometimes lack the data, skill, and other resources--to engage in a systematic, long-range planning process. Thus arises the need for specially trained persons, skilled in the development and organization of health care services and facilities.

Mr. Sieverts stresses that a person pursuing a career in health planning needs skills in the *process* of planning as well as a solid educational background in the *technology* of planning. The latter includes courses in statistics, health economics, research methodology, organizational theory, and health status data. Thus, he emphasizes the need for students to have academic preparation in certain essential fundamentals. Moreover, the health planner needs also to possess "a strong understanding of the realities of management" and have "a solid acquaintance with the appreciation of the clinical side of medical care." In short, planners need to know what institutional managers do and how a hospital functions; they also need to know what doctors and other clinical practitioners do. Like a lawyer who renders advice to a client, the planner must understand the functional features and characteristics of the industry.

Again, a well-constructed course in health law can contribute significantly to both the skills and the knowledge required of the planner. Although the mix of subject matter content and depth of coverage ideally relevant to the planner might vary somewhat from the content most relevant to the institutional manager, both planners and managers can benefit from rigorous analysis of legal cases and contrary opinions. Just as planning involves "a gathering of facts, a testing of assumptions, a forecasting of the future, and a weighing of alternatives," so does the study of law. Lay persons, including, unfortunately, many of our faculty colleagues, do not fully appreciate these characteristics of law when evaluating law courses or the teaching effectiveness of law teachers. It is incumbent on the law instructor to relate his or her professional work to both the skills and the knowledge required of the students. It is also incumbent on the lawyer to integrate the work in law with other courses in the curriculum. The health planning student can benefit with respect to both the process of planning and the acquisition of substantive knowledge pertaining to the functioning of the industry by analyzing legal cases. Legal cases frequently address directly the two questions, What do people do and how do they do it?

A third educational goal of a few master's degree programs is to prepare persons for careers in research and the formulation of public policy. More often than not, a career confined to research will develop after completion of a doctoral degree program. Such programs are beyond the scope of this discussion. Nevertheless, some master's degree programs purport to offer specialization in health policy leading to employment as a policy analyst.

Such positions are limited in number. Some opportunities exist from time to time with state or federal legislative committees or government agencies. Private consulting firms also are interested in persons skilled in research and policy analysis, since they are frequently called on to draft proposals for legislation and administrative regulation or to interpret existing legislation. Since policymaking is a political function operating within all the customary political restraints, these students have a particular need for solid academic course work in political science, the legislative process, and economics. They also need to know the legal and regulatory aspects of health care delivery.

Thus, in summary, at least three or four different, although somewhat overlapping, educational objectives--and, correspondingly, career paths--have been identified:

institutional management, health planning, management consulting, and health policy analysis. Employment opportunities exist for all these career paths with a wide variety of both private and public (government) organizations and agencies.

To these basic career paths should be added two other opportunities and needs in the health industry: health insurance administration and public health administration. Blue Cross and Blue Shield plans, commercial insurance companies, and state and federal governments need persons skilled in the financing of health care. So do the multi-institutional providers now entering the health insurance market. Not often do academic programs purport to train students specifically as health insurance company executives, yet some graduates seek employment and have satisfying careers in this area.

It would appear that a limited number of programs in health administration, both graduate and undergraduate, have focused on the training of public health administrators as a specific educational goal. For our purposes here, a "public health administrator" is a person employed by a local government or state public health department. Traditionally, the public health administrator has been a professional clinician (a physician or nurse) who left active practice to become an administrator. Also, departments of public health have historically had a role limited to, for example, enforcement of licensing regulations for certain businesses serving the public, that is, restaurants, policing of the quality of water and air, the administering of public immunization programs, and the like.

Currently, many local government departments of public health are expanding their influence and increasing their range of activities. Specifically, health departments in some communities are actually providing medical care, thereby becoming, in effect, competitors of other entities. At the state level, public health departments have a leading role in the planning process, seeking to rationalize and coordinate availability and accessibility of a wide range of services. As a consequence, government departments of public health have an increasing need for persons trained formally as institutional managers or health planners. Accordingly, programs that identify public health administration as a specific career goal should advise students to pursue many of the same core-discipline courses typically required of those persons preparing for careers in management or planning, including health law. The law course for such students should not be restricted to the legal dimensions of regulating the environment.

PURPOSES AND OBJECTIVES OF INSTRUCTION IN HEALTH LAW

The foremost objective of a course in health law for a non-law student is to provide a framework for analysis and sufficient knowledge of legal principles to enable the student to recognize legal issues that arise in managerial decision making. Basic knowledge of the law and an accurate understanding of the law's implications convey in some degree to the lay administrator the probable impact of administrative action nor inaction. In short, one can be neither a provider or an administrator of health care without having an understanding of the legal dimensions of his or her professional activity. Today the law is everywhere, and persons must be cognizant of their legal rights and responsibilities as they go about their daily activities.

To accomplish the foregoing objective, the course must describe the structure of the dual court system in the United States (state and federal), fundamental notions of both criminal and civil procedure, and the process of legal reasoning. Unfortunately, the nation's high schools and undergraduate colleges have not provided a sufficient educational experience with respect to the structure of the Anglo-American legal system, the interrelationship of branches of government, and fundamental constitutional doctrine. To recognize and be aware of legal rights and responsibilities, one must first be knowledgeable about the American system of adjudication.

Having recognized the legal dimensions of managerial/ administrative decision making, the administrator will hopefully gain an enhanced ability to distinguish those matters that require the attention of professional legal counsel from those that do not. This, then, is the second objective of a course in health law: to train the student to work with professional legal counsel to prevent lawsuits and legal confrontations. Both lay administrators and legal counsel in today's volatile and changing health care industry must continually be aware of the need to practice preventive law. The prospective health care administrator does not need instruction in health law to know that he or she needs an attorney after receiving a summons announcing that a formal lawsuit has actually been filed. However, the administrator does need to be educated as to what can and should be done on both a short- and long-range basis to prevent legal entanglements. The institutional administrator and also the individual provider of health care should be working systematically with counsel in the development of policies and practices that minimize adversarial relationships.

This is not to say that a professional person in health care must be so fearful that no managerial/administrative decisions are made without a lawyer's specific approval: quite the contrary. If the administrator knows when a lawyer's advice is needed to plan and implement health care programs or services, and when advice is not needed, then he or she is a better administrator. Moreover, since health care institutions are employing in-house counsel to an increasing extent, there are more frequent opportunities for administrative personnel to work regularly and systematically with attorneys.

The third objective flows from the second. It is to communicate the nature of an attorney's discipline, to inform the lay person of what an attorney must do--read and study in order to give informed advice--and to explain the limitations of the law in making managerial decisions and in formulating policy. Lay persons often think or assume that a "yes" or "no" answer is possible for every legal question. They want an attorney to say "Yes, you can do what you propose" or "No, do not do that." Study of legal materials and law review articles quickly dispels the notion that counsel should always be able to render unequivocal advice. Judicious teaching and careful implementation of course requirements can enhance the nonlawyer's understanding of counsel's role and the limitations on a lawyer's ability to predict the future.

A fourth objective is to relate the law to ethical issues, morality, and public policy. Teachers of law should be willing and able to discuss with students the monumental ethical issues confronting health care providers in the light of technological progress, inflationary costs of care, and scarce resources. Moreover, faculty should be prepared to weigh and balance issues of public policy by responding, for example, to the question of whether vigorous enforcement of antitrust legislation is the most effective means of ensuring access to quality of health care at an affordable price. In short, to simply recite antitrust law or the rule that a competent adult patient has the right to refuse medical treatment is not enough. Today's students want guidance on ethical matters, as well as the law, and on how the law relates to ethics.

In conclusion, none of the four objectives strive to train a student of health care administration to make legally significant decisions independent of counsel or to act as his or her own lawyer. The student must be aware that sometimes "a little knowledge is a dangerous thing" and must be reminded that it is prudent to refrain from jumping to conclusions. Although a little knowledge may sometimes be risky if its limits are not recognized, this is no reason to refrain from teaching law to non-law students. A well-taught course can open eyes to issues and legally significant events that have not been seen or appreciated previously and can impart knowledge and skills that professional persons serving the health care industry need to have.

CONTENT OF GRADUATE COURSES IN HEALTH LAW

It is now appropriate to review possible subject matter content of health law course(s) and to relate the subject matter to the several educational objectives and career opportunities identified in the previous discussion. Frequent reference will be made to data gathered by the task force from the Health Law Teachers Survey.

Graduate students in health administration are capable of studying and understanding specific legal applications to the institutional setting, such as those enumerated above, without having completed a business law course in contracts, torts, or business organizations. One need not, for example, fully appreciate the need for consideration as an element of an enforceable contractual obligation or the capacity of a minor to contract in order to study profitably the granting/denial of medical staff privileges and the legal validity of exclusive hospital contracts for professional services. Thus, a graduate level health law course oriented toward institutional management needs no academic prerequisites other than those courses normally required for admission to the degree program.

In discussing course content it is appropriate to categorize legal subject areas in terms of "private" or "public" law. Those areas of law that define the responsibilities and rights of individuals and private organizations among themselves are included within the realm of private law. In contrast, public law embraces those areas of law that create and define the relationship between individuals (and private organizations) and their local, state, and federal governments.

Thus, private law includes the general and traditional areas of contracts, agency, business organizations, commercial transactions, sales, and tort law. More specifically, in the context of health law, private law includes all and more of the following: intentional torts, strict liability, negligence and malpractice, vicarious and corporate liability, medical staff privileges, physician contracts, right to treatment, consent to treatment, and confidentiality of medical or private information. The list of specific applications of the law of contracts and tort to the health care industry is nearly endless.

Public law includes all aspects of constitutional, criminal, and administrative law. Thus, tax law and the vast fields of federal and state regulation have been traditionally characterized as public law. In the areas of hospital-health law, public law includes federal health-planning legislation; state certificate-of-need statutes; Hill-Burton free-care obligations; licensure of individuals and institutions; an individual's right to constitutional due process of law and equal protection in medical contexts; regulation of Blue Cross, Blue Shield, and commercial insurance; Medicare/Medicaid reimbursement; state rate setting; and public health law. Also included are several areas of federal legislation that apply to business generally: the Sherman Act and other antitrust laws, the National Labor Relations Act, the Fair Labor Standards Act, the Civil Rights Act of 1964 and other legislation proscribing discriminatory treatment, the Occupational Safety and Health Act, and legislation regulating the issuance of securities.

The major dilemma, however, for faculty teaching graduate-level courses to students of health administration is this: What is the proper mix of course content between the private and public law subject matter areas? First and foremost, it would seem that all students--regardless of career path--should have a thorough grounding in the Anglo-American legal system, the American court system, and the process of legal reasoning. One cannot appreciate the role of common law decision making, the interaction of the courts, legislative bodies, and administrative agencies, and the roles of the state and federal courts without first studying these fundamental, introductory matters. It was surprising to the task force that only 36 percent of those instructors responding to the survey rated these introductory topics as "very important." Another 41 percent rated them as "moderately important." In any event, all that follows in a course stressing private law subject areas flows from an adequate introduction to the common law system.

The future administrator of a health care organization then needs academic study of corporate law, including the tax-exempt status of the charitable corporation; the development, organization, and legal problems of multi-institutional systems; the legal aspects of hospital-physician relationships and peer review of clinical performance; tort liability to patients and other third parties; consent to treatment; confidentiality of medical information; and the rendering of emergency medical care. Most of these topical matters fall essentially within the area of private law, with, however, statutory and constitutional dimensions. An in-depth, analytic discussion of each of these major topics and their relevance to institutional managerial practices and policies easily consumes a three-credit-hour semester course (three hours per week for 14 weeks) or four hours per week on a quarterly academic calendar.

The following percentages of instructors responding to the Health Law Teachers Survey awarded the rating of "very important" to the topics and subtopics noted below:

Liability (vicarious and corporate)	85
Consent for treatment	83
Confidentiality	78
Refusal to consent and termination of treatment	73
Hospital-physician relationships	66
Emergency care	51
Risk management	49
Corporate law	46
Physicians contracts	34
Multi-institutional systems and corporate reorganizations	31
Antitrust law	29
Peer review	22
Tax law	15

Some of these data are apparently and surprisingly inconsistent. For example, 85 percent of the respondents rank liability issues as very important, while only 49 percent give a similar rank to risk management. It would seem to the task force that liability matters cannot and should not be discussed in class without also giving major attention to risk management and quality assurance programs. If one of the essential purposes of a course in health law for nonlawyers is to emphasize the importance of managerial policy that prevents lawsuits, the management of risks is an essential topic for inclusion in the course.

In the same fashion, two-thirds of the respondents ranked medical staff practice privilege issues as very important. Only a third ranked "physician contracts" as very important, while even fewer gave that rating to antitrust law and the legal aspects of peer review. Again, how can a study of the institution-physician relationship be truly meaningful for the institutional manager unless practice privileges, exclusive contracts, antitrust implications, and the insitution's rights and responsibilities to require peer review are all included?

Forty-six percent of the instructors ranked corporate law as very important, yet course work in multi-institutional systems and corporate reorganization, including antitrust law, was similarly rated by only 30 percent of the respondents. Again, the question that can legitimately be asked is: Should not students be aware that the growth of multi-systems and efforts to diversify corporate activities to generate additional revenue raise issues of corporate law (*ultra vires* and the doctrine of piercing the corporate veil, for example), issues of antitrust, and questions of tax-exempt status? Most surprisingly--and a matter of some concern--only 15 percent of faculty ranked tax law as very important, with another 27 percent awarding a "moderately important" rating to this subject. Thus, more than 50 percent of survey respondents regard tax law as being of little or no importance. This is a matter of concern to the task force for the straightforward reason that corporate structure and diversification of corporate activities (including joint ventures with physicians) raise serious issues of maintenance of tax-exempt status and the taxability of unrelated business income. Managers need to be aware of the tax-law implications of their decisions to reorganize and diversify, they need to be able to communicate with their attorneys, and they need to face and decide the ultimate issue of maintaining current tax status, be it taxable or tax-exempt.

The survey results may, of course, be influenced by the school in which the course is taught. Of the 41 responses, 14 came from schools of allied health, 8 from various "graduate schools," 3 from medical schools, 3 from "other" schools, and 13 from schools of business and public health combined. Faculty of graduate, allied health, and medical schools may have quite a different orientation to health law instruction than faculty of business or public health schools, even though all may have law degrees. Yet, instructors, regardless of the school in which the health administration program resides, should plan the course to fit the educational objectives and career paths of the students. It is thus submitted that all persons preparing for careers in mid- or senior-level institutional management, at least at the graduate level, need academic work in the private law topics and subtopics itemized above, including those that are given a relatively low rating of importance by the majority of health law teachers surveyed.

Institutional managers also need to study legal cases and materials classified as public law: constitutional and administrative law, including principles of federal government regulation, licensure, federal-state relationships, and state regulation of insurance rates and provider reimbursement. These matters are the heart and soul of the future of the health care industry. Regulation and planning of health facilities are here to stay, in spite of the current economic-political philosophy favoring a competitive environment and encouraging enforcement of antitrust legislation. And it is these matters that mid- and senior-level executives (and health planners) read about daily in the trade press and are most concerned about in their day-to-day decision making. As the cost of care continues to escalate, both regulators and free enterprisers are having their day in hearings before administrative agencies and in courtroom litigation. Yet none of these public law topics was rated as high in importance in the Health Law Teachers Survey as the tort and contract principles of law. The highest rank was attained by Medicare/Medicaid reimbursement, which 56 percent of the 41 respondents ranked as "very important." The closely related matter, "DRG's" (diagnosis-related groups), was considered very important by 44 percent of faculty. Only one-third thought that administrative agency process was very important, although 46 percent considered the general topic of constitutional law to be more than moderately important. Licensure of physicians was highly important to 44 percent while licensure of nonphysicians was rated very important by 31 percent. Similarly, all the following topics ranked below 50 percent: principles of governmental regulation and legislative process (41 percent), facility licensing (39 percent), Bill of Rights (39 percent), certificate-of-need legislation (39 percent), National Labor Relations Act (39 percent), and regulation of insurance and government rate setting (34 percent). Significantly, antitrust law, preferred provider organizations, mental health care, problems of capital financing, administration of long-term-care facilities, and hospitals' Hill-Burton Act free-care obligations were given "very important" ratings by less than one-third of the faculty. These are astonishing data in light of the current economic, political, and legal problems confronting the health care industry.

Not surprisingly, however, a number of topics itemized on the Health Law Teachers Survey were rated as having little or no importance. These included rules of evidence, criminal law, bankruptcy, lobbying, international comparative law, human experimentation, guardianships, sterilization, and legal aspects of home health care. Sterilization, for example, might well be covered when discussing consent and therefore would not justify a high ranking of importance on its own merits. The same can be said for home health care law. As costs of institutional care escalate, the principles of law primarily relevant to home health care could well be covered during the study of medical and nursing malpractice. Hence, the task force concurs with the low ranking assigned to these topics.

Ideally, graduate students anticipating careers as managers of health care institutions should complete a two-semester or three-quarter sequence of health law courses. In order to cover adequately the general areas of both private and public law considered significant and relevant to the health administration student, it would seem that approximately 80 classroom contact hours are a legitimate expectation for inclusion in the curriculum.

In similar fashion, it is submitted that students seeking careers in health planning, management consulting, health care policy, and public health administration could likewise benefit substantially from a two-course sequence as suggested for the student anticipating a day-to-day managerial position. It is not academically wise or at all practical to have separate law courses for these several diverse career paths. Substantive concepts and rules of law are the same for managers, planners, and policymakers.

On the other hand the content of health law courses will be and should be influenced by the program's university setting, by the primary educational objectives of the faculty, and by the career aspirations of the majority of the students. In other words, some programs may emphasize graduate training for, say, health planning and/or policymaking in apparent preference to institutional management. Students in planning, consulting, and policymaking may require a greater emphasis in the health law course(s) in subject matter characterized previously as public law: constitutional law, administrative law, government regulation, antitrust, and the legal aspects of Medicare/Medicaid reimbursement, for example. In short, whenever choices of subject matter content must be made, persons engaged in long-range planning and consulting can be well aware of the legal dimensions of their professional responsibilities without a detailed analysis of such private law topics as, for instance, refusal of a patient to consent to medical treatment and medical malpractice. Accordingly, each instructor has the obligation to structure his or her courses and allocate subject matter content consistent with program objectives and employment opportunities of the program's students.

Furthermore, it is certainly recognized that many programs in health administration cannot afford the "luxury" of a two-course sequence recognized as the ideal. Indeed, perhaps most programs will be able to offer only one course in health law. A single course could be either a three-credit (approximately 40 contact hours) or a four-credit (approximately 60 hours) offering. Restraints on the academic contact hours available for health law may be imposed by limited financial resources, unavailability of qualified faculty, or a decision to emphasize/expand instruction in other academic disciplines. Again, of course, the faculty person with responsibility for teaching law must consult with the program director, faculty colleagues, and students to determine the most appropriate credit-hour allocation and the health law course content, taking into account the program's educational objectives and the probable career aspirations of the students.

Presented below are four possible health law course outlines for graduate programs using a semester academic calendar. The first is a three-credit-hour course entitled Law of Health Care Administration; the second course, intended as a sequel to the first, is entitled Government Regulation of the Health Services Industry. The third and fourth course outlines recognize that a two-course sequence may not be possible or practical. Hence, course outline number 3 recommends subject matter content for a single three-credit-hour course, while course number 4 recognizes that four semester hours may be available at some universities. These suggested course outlines could, of course, be readily adjusted to conform to an academic calendar based on the quarter system. On a program-by-program basis, appropriate adjustments should be made for those schools that emphasize training persons for careers in health planning and health care policy as distinct from institutional management.

EXAMPLE COURSES

Course 1

Title: Law of Health Care Administration

Graduate Level - First Semester
42 One-Hour Sessions
Three Credit Hours

Topic   *Hours*

I.   Introduction to Law: Nature, Sources,
     Classifications of Law; Court Systems;
     Powers and Functions of Courts; Judicial
     and Administrative Process; Alternate
     Methods of Resolving Disputes   8

II. Corporate Law: Nature and Characteristics
     of a Corporation, Powers and Authority,
     Corporate Reorganization, Fiduciary Duties
     of Governing Board   2

     A. Nonprofit Status, Charitable Status,
         Federal and State Taxation; Implications
         of Corporate Reorganization   2

     B. Corporate Management: Authority of
         Officers and Agents   2

     C. Antitrust Legislation; Implications of
         Corporate Reorganization and Development
         of Multihospital Systems   2
                                                  Subtotal   8

III. Contract and Tort Law; Creation of
     Relationships   2

     Intentional Torts, Strict Liability, Negligence,
     Professional Malpractice, Standards of Care   2

     Arbitration; Statutory Reforms of Tort System   2

Consent for Treatment, Adults and Minors 2

Withdrawal of Consent, Termination of Treatment 2

Medical Records; Confidentiality 2
                               Subtotal 12

IV. Patient Access to Institutional Care; Emergency Care; Discharge From Care; Impact of Medicare; DRG Reimbursements 2

Institutional Liability to Patients and Visitors, Corporate and Vicarious 4
                               Subtotal 6

V. Physician Access to Hospitals; Medical Staff Appointments and Delineation of Practice Privileges; Public and Private Hospitals 2

Access of Allied Professional Practitioners to Hospitals 1

Relationship of Medical Staff to Hospital; Medical Staff Bylaws 1

Termination of Appointments and Discipline of Professional Staff; Common Law and Constitutional Due Process Rights; Antitrust Litigation; Medical Staff Privileges 2

Risk Management and Quality Assurance Programs; Confidentiality of Records and Immunity of Participants 2
                               Subtotal 8

Total: 42 Class Hours

Course 2

Title: Government Regulation of the Health Services Industry

   Graduate Level - Second Semester
   42 One-Hour Sessions
   Three Credit Hours
   Suggested as a sequel to Course 1

Topic   *Hours*

  I. Constitutional Law; Bill of Rights; Administrative Agencies; Process of Government Regulation of Business; Substantive and Procedural Rights   10

 II. Antitrust Legislation: Sherman, Clayton, Robinson-Patman, Federal Trade Commission Acts   2
     Demise of Jurisdictional Exclusions and Exemptions   2

     Antitrust Implications and Current Status of
       Certificate-of-Need Legislation
       Voluntary Coalitions and Community Planning of Health Services
       Sharing of Services and Group Purchasing Arrangements
       Blue Cross/Blue Shield Participating Provider Contracts
       Preferred Provider Contractual Arrangements
       Peer Review of Necessity and Quality of Care
       Acquisitions and Mergers of Health Care Institutions
       Medical Staff Privileges
       Joint Ventures with Physicians and Other Entities
       Purchase of Drugs or Goods at a Discount
       Restrictions on Advertising and Other Ethical Codes   6
                                           Subtotal   10

III. Employer-Employee Relationships

    Demise of Common Law Employment-at-Will Doctrine   1

    Licensing of Professionals; Scope of Practice   1

    Fair Labor Standards Act; Wages and Hours; Equal Pay Act   2

    Fair Employment, Civil Rights Act, Title VII, as Amended by Pregnancy Act   4

    Fair Employment, Affirmative Action and Comparable Worth   1

    Age Discrimination Act   1

    Rehabilitation Act   1

    Occupational Health and Safety Act   1

    National Labor Relations Act - Duty to Bargain; Bargaining Units   2

    National Labor Relations Act - Unfair Labor Practices by Employers and Unions   2

    Subtotal   14

IV. Financing Health Services

    Regulation of Commercial Insurance   2

    Regulation of Blue Cross/Blue Shield Plans; Conversion to Mutual Insurance Companies   2

    Medicare, Medicaid Reimbursement; Diagnosis Related Group Reimbursement; Fraud and Abuse   2

    State Regulation of Hospital Rates   2

    Subtotal   8

Total: 42 Class Hours

Course 3

Title: Legal Aspects of the Health Services Industry

Graduate Level
42 One-Hour Sessions
Three Semester Credit Hours

Topic *Hours*

I. Introduction to Law: Nature, Sources, Classifications of Law; Court Systems; Powers and Functions of Courts; Judicial and Administrative Process 4

II. Corporate Law: Nature and Characteristics of a Corporation, Powers and Authority, Corporate Reorganization, Fiduciary Duties of Governing Board 2

    A. Nonprofit Status, Charitable Status, Federal and State Taxation; Implications of Corporate Reorganization 2

    B. Corporate Management: Authority of Officers and Agents 2
        Subtotal 6

III. Contract and Tort Law; Creation of Relationships 2

    Intentional Torts, Strict Liability, Negligence, Professional Malpractice, Standards of Care 2

    Arbitration; Statutory Reforms of Tort Systems 1

    Consent for Treatment, Adults and Minors 2

    Withdrawal of Consent, Termination of Treatment 2

    Medical Records; Confidentiality 1
        Subtotal 10

IV. Patient Access to Institutional Care; Emergency
     Care; Discharge from Care; Impact of Medicare;
     DRG Reimbursements   2

     Institutional Liability to Patients and Visi-
     tors, Corporate and Vicarious; Risk Management
     and Quality Assurance Programs   4
                                    Subtotal   6

V.   Physician Access to Hospitals; Medical Staff
     Appointments and Delineation of Practice
     Privileges; Public and Private Hospitals   2

     Access of Allied Professional Practitioners
     to Hospitals   1

     Relationship of Medical Staff to Hospital;
     Medical Staff Bylaws   1

     Termination of Appointments and Discipline of
     Professional Staff; Common Law and Constitu-
     tional Due Process Rights   2
                                    Subtotal   6

VI. Antitrust Legislation: Sherman, Clayton,
     Robinson-Patman, Federal Trade Commission Acts   2

     Antitrust Implications and Current Status of:
       Voluntary Coalitions and Community Planning
         of Health Services
       Blue Cross, Blue Shield Participating Provider
         Contracts
       Preferred Provider Contractual Arrangements
       Peer Review of Necessity and Quality of Care
       Acquisitions and Mergers of Health Care
         Institutions
       Medical Staff Privileges
       Joint Ventures with Physicians and Other
         Entities   4
                                    Subtotal   6

VII. Financing Health Services

   Medicare, Medicaid Reimbursement; Diagnosis
   Related Group Reimbursement; Fraud and Abuse   3

   State Regulation of Hospital Rates   1

   Subtotal   4

   Total: 42 Class Hours

Course 4

Title: Legal Aspects of the Health Services Industry

Graduate Level
60 One-Hour Sessions
4 Semester Hours

Topic   *Hours*

I. Introduction to Law: Nature, Sources, Classifications of Law; Court Systems; Powers and Functions of Courts; Judicial and Administrative Process; Constitutional Law   6

II. Corporate Law: Nature and Characteristics of a Corporation, Powers and Authority, Corporate Reorganization, Fiduciary Duties of Governing Board   2

    A. Nonprofit Status, Charitable Status, Federal and State Taxation; Implications of Corporate Reorganization   2

    B. Corporate Management: Authority of Officers and Agents   2

Subtotal   6

III. Contracts and Tort Law; Creation of Relationships   2

      Intentional Torts, Strict Liability, Negligence,
Professional Malpractice, Standards of Care   2

      Arbitration; Statutory Reforms of Tort Systems   2

      Consent for Treatment, Adults and Minors   2

      Withdrawal of Consent, Termination of Treatment 2

      Medical Records; Confidentiality   <u>2</u>
                           Subtotal 12

IV. Patient Access to Institutional Care; Emergency
Care; Discharge from Care; Impact of Medicare;
DRG Reimbursements   2

     Institutional Liability to Patients and
Visitors, Corporate and Vicarious   <u>4</u>
                           Subtotal 6

V. Physician Access to Hospitals; Medical Staff
Appointments and Delineation of Practice
Privileges; Public and Private Hospitals   2

     Access of Allied Professional Practitioners to
Hospitals   1

     Relationship of Medical Staff to Hospital;
Medical Staff Bylaws   1

     Termination of Appointments and Discipline of
Professional Staff; Common Law and Constitutional
Due Process Rights; Antitrust Litigation -
Medical Staff Privileges   2

     Risk Management and Quality Assurance Programs;
Confidentiality of Records and Immunity of
Participants   <u>2</u>
                           Subtotal 8

VI. Employer-Employee Relationships

    Doctrine Demise of Common Law
Employment-at-Will   1

    Licensing of Professionals; Scope of Practice   1

    Fair Employment Legislation: Affirmative
Action and Comparable Worth   4

    Occupational Health and Safety Act $\underline{2}$

                                Subtotal   8

VII. Antitrust Legislation: Sherman, Clayton, Robinson-Patman, Federal Trade Commission Acts   2

    Antitrust Implications and Current Status of:
      Voluntary Coalitions and Community Planning
        of Health Services;
      Blue Cross/Blue Shield Participating Provider
        Contracts;
      Preferred Provider Contractual Arrangements;
      Peer Review of Necessity and Quality of Care;
      Acquisitions and Mergers of Health Care
        Institutions;
      Medical Staff Privileges;
      Joint Ventures with Physicians and Other
        Entities; $\underline{2}$

                                Subtotal   6

                   Total: 60 Class Hours

NOTES:

1. The Report of the Commission on Education for Health Administration, Volume 1, Health Administration Press, Ann Arbor, Michigan, 1975, page 36.

2. *The Challenge of Administering Health Care Services, Career Pathways*, Bellin and Weeks, Editors, AUPHA Press, Washington, D.C., 1981, page 37. Mr. Sieverts cites Breslow and Spomers, "One Lifetime Health Monitoring Program: A Practical Approach to Preventive Medicine," *New England Journal of Medicine*, 796 (March 17, 1977):601-8.

CHAPTER 5

BACCALAUREATE PROGRAMS IN HEALTH ADMINISTRATION:
HEALTH LAW EDUCATION

If a little knowledge is dangerous, where is the man
who has as much as to be out of danger?

Thomas Huxley, *On Elemental
Instruction in Physiology* (1877)

Over the past two decades, an ample supply of graduates has emerged from undergraduate programs in health administration. In contrast with the relatively well-entrenched graduate education in this field, baccalaureate programs have been the target of considerable uncertainty and debate by practitioners and academics alike. Who are the graduates of such programs? Where are they most likely to be employed? Are they substantially different from graduate students in the same field? Will they continue their education in master's degree programs in health administration? Answers to all of these questions determine the nature of health law education and the manner in which courses are taught.

To assess intelligently the issue of whether universal recommendations are advisable, or even possible, a logical first step is an awareness of the academic programs on the undergraduate level, the profile of students who attend such programs, and the trends in employment of the graduates. This foundation appears in the first part of this chapter, followed by a discussion of objectives, content, and methods of teaching health law to undergraduates.

Undergraduate health administration programs, like their graduate counterparts, are housed in a variety of academic settings. According to AUPHA data, 45 percent of the programs are located within allied health or health professions units, 18 percent in schools or departments of business administration, and 16 percent in community service divisions. Interdisciplinary and "other" settings constitute 8 percent and 12 percent, respectively.[1]

A reasonable inference from this diversity in setting is that the individual program will probably reflect the academic mission of the larger division. On a basic level, then, the objectives and content of health law education should fit the broader goals. Therefore, to prescribe a single generic course formula for all programs may be an exercise in futility.

In 1981, AUPHA conducted a survey of graduates of programs in health administration leading to a bachelor of science or other undergraduate degree.[2] These graduates, a representative sample from programs in the United States and Canada, were asked to provide information on, among other things, personal characteristics, health-related employment, and perceptions on required education for satisfactory performance on the job. Because the results from the survey may shed light on the prospects for employment of the students, and because the survey lends a very generalized impression of the subject of health law education, a summary of selected findings provides the groundwork for the subsequent discussion of course objectives, content, methods, and materials.

Respondents to the survey fell into two classifications with regard to age at time of graduation: 21-23 year olds (60 percent), and 25-39 year olds (25 percent), with the remainder scattered across the continuum from 20 to over 50 years of age. Forty seven percent of these graduates had less than three years of health-related employment or none, while 40 percent indicated a 5- to 20- year history of the same background. Sixty percent of the total responding held only the undergraduate degree in health administration, and 29 percent had one other degree (diploma, associate, or other bachelor's), with nursing the most frequently cited field of study. Fewer than one-fourth (15 percent) were M.H.A. or similar degree graduates, and 6 percent stated that they had completed an M.B.A. degree at the time of the survey.

Sixty-seven percent of the total said that they were employed in the health field. Within that percentage, positions were delineated as follows:[3]

	Percent
CEO (Administrator, Executive Director, President)	12
Assistant/Associate (Administrator, Director, Vice President)	9
Administrative Assistant/Clerk/Resident	7
Department/Unit: Director/Supervisor	30
Clinical Staff	12
Support Staff (non-clinical)	12
Research Staff	5
Health Planner	5
Sales/Consulting	4
Other	4

Forty two percent of those employed in the health field were in hospitals, 13 percent in nursing homes, and another 13 percent in ambulatory care settings. Smaller percentages were found in planning bodies, foundations or associations, health departments, and educational organizations.

Asked to describe the primary areas of responsibility in these positions, 34 percent designated general administration, 21 percent organizational or institutional planning, and 21 percent personnel management.[4]

Although the survey furnished no specific information on attitudes toward health law within the completed curriculum, general replies were gathered on the relative importance of the subject to graduates employed in the health field. A mere 6 percent selected health law (defined as "legal concepts and regulation within the health area") as a most beneficial area, in contrast with the highest-rated categories of applied administration and management with a health care emphasis and general business, which both received 25 percent ratings in this category. None, however, thought that health law was least beneficial;

and when queried whether the subject deserves greater depth in the health administration curriculum, 8 percent responded affirmatively.[5]

Several limitations should be noted before using these broad-brush responses to decide upon objectives, content, and methods. The nature, scope, and quality of the instruction were not ascertained in the survey, and students could have been assessing a health law course or, alternatively, scattered pieces of health law throughout various courses. It is not unreasonable to assume, for example, that a program would limit study of health law to planning law or licensure requirements within the state. In addition, it is unclear whether the students were rating the quality of their exposure to health law in terms of the subject matter or, rather, according to the merits or demerits of a particular instructor. Conclusions from the general statements should be drawn with extreme caution. Nevertheless, the survey lends some value to our immediate task; we may at least make a beginning by designing a course to meet the requirements of a conceptualized "typical" undergraduate student.

OBJECTIVES AND CONTENT OF HEALTH LAW

As seen above, we have at least some vague notion of the "average" undergraduate student in health administration. He or she is either the traditional baccalaureate student in terms of age, or is a bit older with a strong likelihood of prior health care experience in the workplace. A healthy percentage of graduates employed in the health field are in hospitals, in middle management. Some--but a clear minority at the time of the survey--continued academically to attain a master's degree, either in health or business administration.

If a health law course is tailored for the mid-management hospital position, some generalizations are possible about health law objectives and content--potentially quite different from a course within a program that routinely produces students to fill top administrative positions.

We may assume, for example, that a mid-level manager in a health care institution requires less knowledge about relating to lawyers than a CEO or vice president. Further, a deep understanding of the law's more abstract philosophical underpinnings is probably not necessary. Objectives for a health law course are more realistically tied to a familiarity with relevant basic legal principles and issues--a familiarity that would enable a middle-manager to recognize potential legal difficulties and suggest prudent protective methods within the day-to-day demands of employment. A second objective would be to convey a modicum of knowledge about the changing nature of rulings, legislation, and their applications in the field.

A separate but related question is whether the outcome of the course should be a preparedness to recognize basic business issues without a particular health focus (e.g., those based in contract, the Union Commercial Code, agency, and so on) or the more focused health care legal issues (e.g., exclusive contracts in hospitals, malpractice, and informed consent, to name but a few topical areas).[6]

The difficulty with the former approach in instructing undergraduates lies in the use of examples. Business law, as typically taught, may have little or nothing to do with the actual experience the graduate has on the job. He or she may be at the level of administrative department head, but a position in nursing or radiology, for example, requires the need to recognize a basic informed consent problem, if not to recommend an approach to be taken to protect the hospital.

Assuming, then, that a health law (rather than general business law) approach is preferable in educating any prospective management employee, what types of subject matter should be included in the course? An atlas of possible material is as follows:

    I. Sources and Types of Law

    II. Corporations

Structure, governance, and management
  Role of medical staff
     Tax status
     Mergers and acquisitions
     Multi-institutional systems

III. Governmental Regulation of Health Care Institutions and Providers
     Police power, commerce clause and constitutional limitations of government power
     Professional licensure
     Institutional licensure
     Antitrust
     Planning legislation/CON
     FDA
     OSHA
     Fair Labor Standards Act
     Workers' compensation and unemployment compensation
     National Labor Relations Act
     Toxic waste

 IV. Patient-Provider Relations
     Formation/termination of relationship
     Admission/discharge
     Emergency care
     Contract actions against providers
     Malpractice/negligence
     Consent issues
     Medical records issues
     Abortion and sterilization

  V. Physician-Institution Relationship
     Medical staff bylaws and organization within the institution
     Medical staff privileges
     Quality assurance issues
     Contracts with physicians for professional and/or administrative services

The above list is not meant to suggest that these topics should replace business law education. Ideally, the student will study both areas, with health law preferably following business law preparation at the undergraduate level. However, the reality in most baccalaureate programs is that students take only the single law course selected for the curriculum.

Three variables require critical attention in determining content. First, the course should be carefully crafted to correspond with the program's individual history of student placement upon graduation. The failure to aim knowledge to the highest administrative level--where warranted--does grave disservice to both the student and to the reputation of the program in the field. Second, the program may have a particular substantive thrust and the content and depth of knowledge should be geared accordingly. For example, several baccalaureate curricula concentrate on nursing home administration. Traditionally these programs are more likely to produce students who will fill the top administrative position--often not long after the date of graduation. Under these circumstances, the topics should reflect the legal issues that arise in a nursing home, as opposed to a hospital, HMO, or medical group practice. Also, the depth of education should be varied from a broadly sweeping course of all health law topics to a more detailed look at the topics selected particularly for those students. Third, the program option of requiring both business law as a prerequisite and a health law course is most strongly recommended where there is an increased likelihood that students will assume top-level management positions upon graduation.

Another type of program decision arises on a more fundamental level. Assuming the bachelor of science degree serves as the student's terminal degree, what is the programmatic responsibility in promoting life-long learning through the undergraduate curriculum in contrast with the more pragmatic preparation for an employment role upon graduation? One approach involves a blending of traditional general education (including history, languages, literature, sciences, and philosophy) with health administration content in more or less equal parts. Another alternative is to concentrate on health administration and business courses at the expense of exposure to broader liberal education. Or, third, this prioritization may be reversed, yielding a greater focus on general education and less on strict health administration topics. Of course, this decision is influenced by a variety of factors, including the university policies on general education requirements and minimum specifications regarding the student's major area of study. Also, AUPHA criteria for undergraduate programs specify the academic content that must be met for program eligibility as AUPHA members. Within these confines, however, there is discretion in the philosophy of baccalaureate education: Should students be prepared solely to enter management positions at the completion of the curriculum? Or should a broader exposure to learning constitute the focus of the program?

METHODS

Having narrowed the objectives and content appropriately, the instructor's next challenge is the selection of methods to meet the goals. While the most familiar teaching style to lawyers is Socratic--in the sense of using questions in the classroom to gain well-reasoned conclusions about the law--the impediment lies in the restricted amount of class time in undergraduate health law study. In most programs, one course is allotted, and often the teacher is saddled with all content areas discussed in the previous pages. Curricula that incorporate some of the listed material in other courses (e.g., labor law, health planning, licensure, and Medicare law) allow more concentrated time for the remaining topics to be addressed. Therefore, methods for teaching depend in large part upon the program's overall curricula. However, it is doubtful that all material will be adequately covered if the Socratic method is used, despite the benefits possible from this style of teaching, specifically, exercise of the faculty of legal reasoning; familiarity with the way in which lawyers and judges think; and greater knowledge of the exceptions to generalized legal principles.

Closely related to the Socratic method as an educational tool is the use of case discussion in class. Difficulties arise here too, since the student is probably encountering legal jargon for the first time in the law course. Undergraduates often express frustration with reading cases for class. It is not unusual to find a bright student totally bewildered about the interplay between trial and appellate courts, even after several readings. The greatest difficulty, however, lies in the technical language--not to mention Latin phrases--and a teacher could spend entire classes on explaining the meaning of motions referenced alone. Although at the end of the course students are more facile in reading and discussing cases, time is the predominant restriction with this method as with Socratic exchange.

There are, however, educational merits in having undergraduate students grapple with court opinions. First, they see as first hand witnesses the judicial application of precedent. Second, the court's willingness to deviate from prior legal rulings is best demonstrated by the reading of opinions. Third, the interaction between legislative enactment and the court's interpretation of the law is best illustrated through an actual fact pattern.

The counterpoint to the Socratic method and case-law teaching is didactic lecture with emphasis on black-letter law. Here a serious danger arises, namely, that health law may appear to the student as static, ingrained and predictable akin to mathematics, where one need only learn certain precepts and later apply them to the particulars at hand. Thus, the constantly changing aspect of law may be lost altogether. The remedy may be the carefully tailored mean between delivering carved-in-stone legal tenets (with, perhaps, a very short shelf life) and delving into the intricacies, exceptions, and dynamic nature of law. One possible tack is a deliberate variation in depth on certain topics. Depending on the objectives carved out for the particular program's students, stress may be placed in class on the more critical areas by use of assigned court opinions and Socratic exchange in class on the material.

A crucial component in the selection of methods for an undergraduate health law course is evaluation tools. Indeed the approach to grading--assuming students are adequately aware of the expectations of the instructor--can reinforce and bolster the objectives and content of the course by encouraging more intensive learning of certain aspects or topics of law.

Testing is the most common evaluation tool, and a threshold decision involves a choice between several "mini" exams throughout the course and/or a mid-term, followed by a final at the completion. Undergraduate students are particularly eager to know "how they are doing," which makes the law school schedule of one examination at the end of the course rather inappropriate. (Part of the uneasiness of these students stems from the broader spread of grades generally given at the undergraduate level than in graduate school.)

Closely linked to this question is the format of the exam. This decision may be most appropriately resolved in accordance with two factors: 1) the instructor's time constraints in grading examinations, and 2) the objectives of the course in terms of focus on memorization of black-letter law versus familiarity with the element of change and complexity of law. On this latter point, essay answers are clearly the evaluation tool of choice, in contrast with multiple choice or a fill-in-the-blank format which more closely matches the former. In favor of essay examinations is the broader educational goal for undergraduate students: fostering the skills of organizing material and cogent writing. Searching for a balance between these two may lead to a combined approach, where the student is tested on the grasp of black-letter law and the capacity to articulate in more depth on a few selected areas.

Pursuing this theme of balance a bit further, research papers are a particularly applicable evaluation device. Students are encouraged to explore the subtleties and intricacies of at least one topic which may, at first blush, appear simple and straightforward. Inherent in this type of exercise is an education in use of a law library; use of law review articles and court opinions and legislation as required bibliographic sources; and the application and sources of law in health care. For health law teachers who assume that such a requirement may be too arduous for undergraduates, experience suggests quite the contrary. Instead of finding law review articles too compendious or detailed, students report less difficulty in deciphering the meaning of these works than in reading a single court opinion. One obstacle to this evaluation method's use is, of course, lack of availability of or access to a law library, either on campus or within a reasonable commuting distance.

Special teaching techniques may also have an important role in teaching health law to undergraduate students, particularly where the student is given firsthand impressions of the law in "real" life (e.g., films of mock trials). Short films displaying the use of medical records in the courtroom may, for instance, more clearly demonstrate the reasons for studying this area. Attendance at actual trials is superb, although logistics of geography, student time, and court dockets may render this infeasible. Because undergraduates have a stronger need than M.H.A. students for comprehending the connection between classroom material and its place in administration, special techniques should be considered for use and selected to accomplish this aim.

ATTACHMENT I

Position Description of Respondents Currently Employed in Health

	Age at Graduation					
	24 Years or Less (n=473)		25 Years or More (n=306)		Respondents (n=780)	
	#	%	#	%	#	%
Position Title						
CEO	41	9	55	18	96	12
Asst./Assoc. Adm.	42	9	28	9	70	9
Admin. Assistant	39	8	18	6	57	7
Dept./Unit Director/Superv.	132	28	100	33	232	30
Clinical Staff	33	7	57	19	90	12
Support Staff	75	16	15	5	90	12
Research Staff	35	7	7	2	42	5
Health Planner	29	6	7	2	36	5
Sales/Consulting	23	5	5	2	23	4
Other	24	5	8	3	32	4
Self-Defined Position Level						
Upper-Level Admin./Mgt.	94	20	81	26	175	23
Middle-Level Admin./Mgt.	161	34	124	41	285	37
Lower-Level Admin./Mgt.	114	24	26	8	146	19
Clinical	27	6	41	13	68	9
Non-Admin./Mgt.	52	1	24	8	66	9
Other	21	4	2	1	23	3

ATTACHMENT II

Primary Areas of Responsibility and Activities/Tasks for Respondents Currently Employed in the Health Field

	Respondents Currently Employed in the Health Field (n=780)
Primary Area of Responsibility*	% Reporting
General Administration	34
Institutional/Organizational Planning	21
Personnel Management	21
Regulation/Compliance	18
Evaluation Program Services	17
Quality Assurance	16
Financial Management	15
Operation Res./Systems Eng.	15
Clinical Services	15
Information Systems	12
Interagency Liaison	12
Health Promotion & Prevention	11
Materials Management	11
Education	10
Fund Raise/Public Relations	8
Marketing	8
Physical Plant Management	8
Accounting	6
Environmental Services	6
Sales	4
Other	9
*Activities/Tasks***	
Intraorganizational Agency Functions (e.g., general administration or research, etc.)	67
Activities Specific to an Organizational Unit (e.g., financial planning, medical records, etc.)	54

Direct Patient/Clinical Services (e.g, nursing, education, sales, etc.)	27
External Organizational Relations (e.g., public relations, community education, etc.)	13
Department/Unit Management (e.g., director personnel, head nurse, etc.)	10
Other	3

* Percentages do not equal 100 due to multiple responses.
**This was an open question with lines allotted for two answers.

ATTACHMENT III

Knowledge and Skill Areas*

	Currently and/or Have Been Employed in Health Field (n=928)	
	Number	% Reporting
MOST BENEFICIAL		
Applied Admin./Org./Mgt. (health emphasis)	237	25
General Business	237	25
Personnel Administration (health emphasis)	182	20
Gen. Admin./Org./Mgt. Theory	160	17
Finan. Mgt. (health emphasis)	147	16
Practicum	151	16
General Education/Liberal Arts	152	16
Communications	132	14
Health Planning	125	13
Quant./Statistics	91	10
Health Care Organization	84	9

Health Law	60	6
Med./Nursing Practice	43	5
Economics	50	5
Applied Org. Psych./Soc.	49	5

LEAST BENEFICIAL

"Liberal Arts"	85	9
General Science (e.g., Bio., Chem.)	82	9
General Business	78	8
Sociology	47	5
History	46	5
Quant./Statistics	45	5

NEEDS GREATER DEPTH

Financial Mgt. (health emphasis)	234	25
General Business	169	18
Applied Admin./Org./Mgt. (health emphasis)	128	14
Personnel Admin. (health emphasis)	105	11
Communications	103	11
Inf. Sys./Computer App.	94	10
Government Relations	87	9
Quant./Statistics	77	8
Health Law	72	8
Gen. Admin./Org./Mgt. Theory	63	7
Health Planning	52	5
Health Care Organization	50	5
Med./Nursing Practice	44	5
Economics	47	5

SHOULD BE INCLUDED

Financial Mgt. (health emphasis)	127	14
General Business	112	12
Communications	105	11

Personnel Admin. (health emphasis)	96	10
Info. Sys./Computer App.	84	9
Government Relations	69	7
Applied Admin./Org./Mgt. (health emphasis)	58	6
Med./Nursing Practice	48	5

*Numbers do not correspond to the total "n" due to multiple responses. Knowledge and skill areas cited by less than 5 percent of the respondents are not reported.

NOTES:

1. AUPHA, *Baccalaureate Health Administration Graduates: A Decade of Review*. Arlington, Va.: AUPHA (1983).

2. *Ibid.*

3. See Attachment 1 for this table and other related data.

4. See Attachment 2 for a more complete listing on this subject.

5. See Attachments 3 and 4.

6. AUPHA membership criteria require health law as part of the curriculum but do not specify the particular areas for inclusion.

CHAPTER 6

TEACHING MATERIALS

Essential to the teaching of any course is the ready availability of useful textbooks and a body of literature in the field. During the past decade, as interest in the issues affecting health law has continued to increase, this area has experienced a proliferation of information sources. The growing body of literature is being produced by both academicians and practitioners for the research and professional journals. This chapter reviews the issues of a textbook versus bulkpack materials, use of copyrighted material, and use of the law library. A selected list of teaching materials is included at the end.

USE OF A TEXTBOOK VERSUS BULKPACK MATERIALS

In any classroom setting, a teacher must decide which materials are appropriate for a particular class. Many factors must be considered when making this decision, and a number of these, such as university rules and the location of the health administration program within the university setting, are discussed elsewhere in this report. The fundamental decision is usually whether to use a textbook or a bulkpack.

Textbooks

The field of health law contains relatively few textbooks with a general approach to the field, but, nevertheless, instructors may find the following factors helpful.

1. *Book Content*. Once the health law teacher has created an outline of the topics sought to be covered in the course, the available textbooks should be examined to determine whether they are compatible with the syllabus. The first item that should be studied is the nature of the content of each book. Are all or most of the syllabus

topics covered? Are the topics arranged in a logical order? Is the material presented in a teachable form? Does the author cite the landmark cases in a particular area and the subsequent development of the law? Does the author use any material that has been developed from statutes? How do the various textbooks compare with one another? These are only a few basic questions that need to be answered when selecting textbooks.

2. *Author*. After studying the contents of a textbook, one must consider the authors. Are they recognized as teachers in the field? Are they recognized as authorities on the subject of health law? Also to be considered are the colleges or universities where the authors are teaching, where they have taught in the past, and whether they have published other textbooks.

3. *Adoptions*. The person selecting the textbook should also explore which other colleges and universities have adopted this particular textbook. Is this a textbook that has been used mainly at the undergraduate or graduate level? What is the opinion of those teachers who have used the text regarding its quality and utility? The publisher's sales representative should be willing and able to provide such information as well as references to faculty currently using the text.

4. *Date of publication or revision*. The date of a textbook, in a field changing as rapidly as health law, should be considered. Any textbook with an old copyright date will not have the latest court decisions or major changes wrought by statute or regulation. Additionally, students may resist purchasing an outdated textbook. (Of course, a recent copyright does not ensure a quality text.)

5. *Writing style*. Another consideration is the writing style of the author. Health law textbooks are written by attorneys, who, like those in other learned professions, tend to write in a very stylized, technical manner. A person selecting a textbook should read several chapters to determine if the language is clear, comprehensible, and interesting. Does the author merely recite the law,

or is it dealt with in a manner that generates discussion and understanding of the material? In other words, is the material presented in a teachable form?

6. *Publisher*. Another factor to consider is the publisher. What is the publisher's reputation in the health administration field? When will the publisher deliver the textbooks once an order has been placed? Has the publisher had trouble meeting delivery dates in the past? How soon will additional orders be filled, and how? Which delivery method will the publisher use to provide a few additional copies of the book, if needed, so that all students will have a textbook from the beginning of the course?

7. *Supplemental materials*. The instructor should also consider the availability of supplemental materials for the textbook. How much support will the publisher give the teacher if the book is adopted? Three basic supplemental materials may accompany textbooks: a teacher's manual, a test bank, and a student study guide (workbook). The teacher's manual is the most important because it will contain the answers to any case questions, chapter-end problems, etc. that the author may have included in the text. It may also contain suggestions on how to teach the chapters, or field experiences to illustrate a particular set of points. The teacher's manual may also contain bibliographies on various topics. Basically, a teacher's manual saves the faculty member time in assembling material with which to teach the class. A test bank of suggested questions is also a timesaver. The questions may serve as a basis for the teacher to create his or her own test questions, and they permit the teacher to make sure the major topics, with subpoints, will be covered by the test. A student study guide allows the student to cover the material at his or her own pace and is particularly useful in supplementing areas which cannot be fully covered in class. A study guide can also be used to reinforce the important points discussed in the textbook.

8. *Price*. The final item to be considered is the price of the textbook. Needless to say, this should be supported by the book's quality. Students, like all con-

sumers, want their money's worth. They especially resent being required to pay for materials that are not used in the course. It is a good idea for teachers to check periodically to be sure that the cost of their course materials is in line with the cost of other course materials.

Bulkpacks

One problem with using textbooks is that no textbook can cover every area within the diverse field of health law. Therefore, the faculty member may choose to supplement certain areas in the course that the textbook does not treat. Bulkpack materials are one way of providing students with materials on topics not adequately covered by the course's main text.

The bulkpack is a compilation by the teacher of various materials that may or may not have been copyrighted. The issue of copyright clearances is addressed later. By compiling a bulkpack, the faculty member has control over the specific materials that the students will be reading. The teacher must have a plan for the selection of the materials to be included in the bulkpack. This plan is similar to the table of contents in a textbook. The following factors may be of use to a person who is assembling materials for a bulkpack.

1. *Goal of the use of bulkpacks*. This must first be established. Basically there are two uses for the bulkpack: (1) in lieu of a textbook and (2) as a supplement to a textbook.

a. *Use in lieu of a textbook*. In this case the bulkpack must be constructed to cover most, if not all, the topics for the quarter or semester. If this is not feasible, then the teacher must have other material on reserve at the library to supplement the bulkpack materials. Construction of the bulkpack must be carefully planned in advance so that the students will have the appropriate materials to study at the designated time. Nothing can dampen students' enthusiasm for a course faster than having materials unavailable when they go to purchase them.

   b. *Use as supplemental material.* Use of a bulkpack as a supplement to a textbook also needs to be carefully considered. The teacher must first determine why the textbook needs to be supplemented. He or she may decide that bulkpack materials could better explain a concept that is too thinly covered in the textbook. For example, the students may benefit from reading an entire case rather than one that is poorly edited in the textbook. A key case in the text may have been revised on appeal or otherwise overturned subsequently, after the text was published. A supplemental bulkpack may also be used to include additional material not covered in the textbook at all. In either event, the teacher must select the bulkpack material carefully and be sure that it is available to the students in a timely manner.

  2. *Selection of materials for the bulkpack.* Once the decision is made to have a bulkpack and the reasons for the decision are clear, the teacher must decide which materials to include. The following are items to consider including in the bulkpack.

   a. *Statutes.* Many areas of health law are governed by statutes, both at the federal and state levels. Selected statutes on a particular topic can be used to illustrate the political process that led to the wording of the statute and the decision to enact a particular statute or a statutory scheme. At the federal level, a wealth of material is easily found on the various Congressional hearings, debates, and committee reports on a statute prior to and, sometimes, after the adoption of the statute. (A caveat is needed here. Although the statute is public, all of the annotated material is copyrighted. The annotated material must not be included in the bulkpack without permission from the publisher.) Note that, while it may be useful for students to have exposure to statutory materials and the legislative process, most statutory materials are very dry and make tedious reading. Student tolerance for substantial doses of such materials is typically very low.

b. *Cases*. Cases, i.e., reported judicial opinions, constitute the bulk of teaching materials in many health law courses. Once they become accustomed to reading cases, students generally enjoy dealing with legal materials in this form. There can be problems, however, in selecting among the overwhelming number of cases available in the health law field. Obviously, a teacher should seriously consider the "landmark" cases that are nationally known. "Local landmarks," i.e., cases recognized within the state where the course is being taught, should also be considered, since students have an understandable and justifiable interest in knowing the law under which they will be functioning. (Clearly, this last point has greater validity in programs that place the bulk of their graduates in a single locality.) Care should be taken, though, to avoid having a focus that is too narrowly local.

Another selection issue to be addressed is whether old or new cases should be used in the teaching materials. Even though the health law field is extremely fast-moving, some cases continue to stand as landmarks long after their date of decision; and a well-reasoned, pivotal decision can be an excellent teaching tool even when it is decades old. A balance must be struck between teaching from the "old favorites" and trying to find cases that are on the "cutting edge" of the law. Given the precedent-based nature of our legal system, giving students a sense of the historical development and flow of the law is very important. Unfortunately, this truth can too easily be used to rationalize continuing to teach from familiar and tired materials when newer cases may have much more to offer. The optimum blending of old and new case materials is a real challenge for the health law teacher. Those who cannot do it--or are unwilling to commit the personal time needed to do well--may be better advised to teach from textbooks and published casebooks.

Once the appropriate mix of cases is chosen, the teacher faces the not inconsiderable chore of editing the cases down to a usable length. For all of their didactic strengths, court opinions tend to be verbose and redundant. Moreover, case opinions often devote significant attention to procedural and ancillary issues that are not relevant to what the teacher wishes to emphasize. There is some value in teaching students how to sift through the "chaff" of court opinions and pull out the key issues and principles. For the most part, however, it is advisable for the teacher to edit the cases down fairly tightly, so the student has little to read except that which is directly relevant to the course. (This is especially true in the case of students, e.g., health administration majors, who are not pursuing a degree in law.) Students have a limited amount of time and energy to devote to their health law course; the teacher should take great care to husband this resource. Moreover, it can be prohibitively expensive to reproduce cases in their entirety. Editing is the answer, but it is tedious and time-consuming work. Some faculty members will have support staff available--secretaries, teaching assistants, etc.--who can handle the mechanical aspects of the editing process. But it is far more common for the teacher to have to do not only the substantive editing but also the physical work of cutting, taping, laying out, etc., the cases to be included in the bulkpack. There is probably no task--with the possible exception of grading--that the teacher finds more burdensome and odious. It is no wonder that teachers--especially part-time faculty members who have very limited time to devote to their teaching activities--have a tendency to put off updating their bulkpacks and, consequently, to teach from stale materials.

A couple of final points should be observed regarding the use of cases: First, it is important to place the cases in a logical sequence within the bulkpack. If three or four cases are to be read for a given class, the order in which they are read generally makes a difference to the student's understanding and appreciation of the mateial. Teachers choose carefully the order in which they present the cases in class; it is no less important to consider the order in which they are arranged in the bulkpack. Second, another copyright caution is appropriate here. Although court opinions are in the public domain, cases edited and published in casebooks are entitled to copyright protection for their headnotes, comments, etc.

Even the editing--that is, the systematic omission of selected parts of the court's opinion--is arguably protected by copyright. "Lifting" edited cases from a published casebook for use in a bulkpack is not without legal risk.

    c. *Law journal articles.* Timely or seminal law journal articles should definitely be considered for inclusion in the bulkpack. Such articles are typically very carefully and thoroughly researched and documented. Although they often speak from a point of view and/or advocate a particular position, they generally are balanced and objective in their presentation. One of the most impressive aspects of the legal discipline, especially observable in its academic branch, is this devotion to objectivity in the presentation of data. Evidence can be seen of this in the standard format of footnotes in law journal articles, citing not only supporting references but also those which favor an opposing position. Students readily come to appreciate law journal articles--and, by extrapolation, to respect the discipline of law--for this objectivity and also for their completeness and comprehensive treatment of topics. Law journals also serve as excellent legal research resources because of their extensive and precise citation format. Most important of all, students generally enjoy reading law journal articles and seem to absorb readily the information presented through this medium.

    A copyright caveat must also be entered here. Law journals are virtually always copyrighted; thus, permission to reprint articles must be obtained unless one of the "fair use" exceptions, discussed later, applies. As a practical matter, law journals, probably because they originate in the academic community, are generally liberal in their grant of reprint permission for educational purposes.

    3. *Price and distribution.* The reproduction of these materials is not cheap even at the subsidized prices available through many universities' duplicating centers. The volume of material also affects the cost of the bulkpack; often a different rate per page is charged when the number of copies ordered exceeds a certain threshold. Bulkpack

materials may be reproduced at the expense of the university; but the more common approach is to sell the bulkpack to the students, university rules permitting, through the faculty member, the bookstore, a copying center, or a publishing house. These reproduction and distribution facilities may be located off campus and, thus, may pose an inconvenience to the teacher and students alike.

Another way of handling the distribution of bulkpacks is to place the materials on reserve at the library. This will reduce, but not eliminate entirely, copyright concerns. If the students regularly make their own copies of the material on reserve, copyright may be infringed. A further disadvantage of the library-reserve method is that occasionally the reserved material will disappear or be damaged to such an extent that it is useless. Moreover, even when the material remains intact, it is generally less used and appreciated by students than when they have their own personal copies of the course materials.

4. *Keeping materials current.* As noted above, a teacher who has decided to use bulkpacks must review the materials on a regular basis to ensure that they are still good law and still applicable. This updating requires a thorough review of the legal literature so that all materials are current, timely, and properly keyed to the course. It is not uncommon for a teacher's class notes to start out closely synchronized with the readings when a course is new or newly revised and then to diverge over time. Ideally, the class experience should be much more than just a verbal rehash of the course's written materials. But if the teacher's presentation and the materials differ much, disparate, students will have greater difficulty seeing the relevance of the readings and may be discouraged from preparing the written material for class. Whenever new materials are added to the bulkpack, appropriate changes in the teacher's lesson plan and lecture notes should be made.

COPYRIGHT ISSUES

Many of the above types of materials generally carry a copyright. An often ignored but highly sensitive challenge is how to use such materials without violating copyright restrictions. Assuming that the material is copyrighted, the health law teacher has available two courses of action. First, the Federal Copyright Act, as amended in 1976, includes a "fair use" provision. The statute sets out four factors for the court to consider in making a decision concerning fair use:

1. What is the purpose and character of the use? Is it of a commercial nature or is it for nonprofit educational purposes?

2. What is the nature of the copyrighted work?

3. What is the amount and substantiality of the portion used in relation to the copyrighted work as a whole?

4. What is the effect of the use on the potential market for, or the value of, the copyrighted work?

A set of guidelines has been agreed on by the Ad Hoc Committee on Copyright Law Revision, representing various educational institutions, on one hand, and the Author-Publisher Group, Authors League of America, and the Association of American Publishers, Inc., on the other hand. Basically, the guidelines allow a teacher to make one copy for his or her scholarly research or use in teaching or preparing to teach a class. The guidelines allow multiple copies, not to exceed one copy per student in the course, to be made if the teacher meets a threefold test: (1) the test of brevity, (2) the test of "spontaneity" and (3) a "cumulative effect" test. Also, each copy must include a notice of copyright. Obviously, substantial repetitive "borrowing" of copyrighted materials fails these tests.

The latitude within which it is safe to copy is a matter of debate in academic circles.

The second way to comply with the Copyright Act is to obtain express permission from the copyright holder to reproduce the copyrighted material. Unfortunately, it is not always clear whether the author or the publisher holds the copyright. Generally, it is the publisher, and usually a request to the publisher to reproduce the material without charge will elicit a response; unfortunately, the response is too often negative or, at best, delayed. Full compliance with the copyright laws, the only safe approach, can require substantial lead time before the course is to be taught.

USE OF THE LAW LIBRARY

Some fortunate health administration programs are near a law library. This greatly eases the burdens discussed above. Moreover, where a library resource is handy, the teacher may assign a legal research project (see Chapter 3 on Teaching Objectives and Methods). The students may use the materials in the law library to prepare a legal research paper and to supplement other parts of the course as well. A valuable educational objective is to teach students enough about legal research and materials that they will feel comfortable in using the law library's many resources.

The above assumes not only that there is a law library close at hand but that the library is willing to extend the use of its facilities and materials to health administration students. On this point, experience varies widely from university to university, and even from teacher to teacher. Some university law libraries are tightly restricted to use by law school students and faculty. This is especially the case where the facilities and staff are already heavily utilized; but even where the resources are not in short supply, there may be a tendency for the law school to want to husband them for the use of their own students. This tendency is understandably increased if the non-law students and faculty do not show appropriate sensitivity to the law school's situation and the constraints and pressures under which it operates. Common sense is the key to establishing and maintaining a good working relationship between the health law teacher and the law librarian so that each party has a clear understanding of the other's role. If the teacher and the librarian communicate well and share common objectives, they can resolve potential problems before they get out of hand. A meeting--or at least a telephone conversation--before the course begins is a useful first step. Arranging a student tour of the law library is also helpful. Such a tour will give the students a sense of how the library is laid out and where research and lending materials may be found and, thus, will ease the burdens on library staff. A problem with having the students use the law library is the danger that they will ask the librarians so many questions that the librarians are, in effect, conducting the research instead of the student. The students must be cautioned against misusing library staff. A proper working arrangement should include having the librarian report to the faculty member any students who abuse the privilege of access to legal research assistance.

SUMMARY

The above discussion about how to approach the selection and use of various types of teaching materials focuses on the general factors a health law teacher should consider. The difficulties involved in identifying timely and functional materials are compounded by the cost and convenience barriers of access and availability. The location and resources of a health administration program cannot be expected to support the complete range of desirable options in materials selection. Too few programs have a law library close by and students cannot be expected to buy all of the books and materials that the teacher would like them to use. Therefore, care must be exercised in deciding which materials to acquire for health law teaching. The health administration program can greatly enhance the health law teacher's effectiveness by providing a library and course materials allowance. (See Chapter 2.)

SELECTED LIST OF TEACHING MATERIALS

To assist health law teachers in appreciating the wealth of currently available materials, a catalogue of materials can be found in the appendix following Chapter 9. Because of the wide range of subject matter included in various definitions of health law and because of the dynamic nature of the publishing field, this list contains only selected items.

This list was prepared by the professional staff of the Duke University Law Library in conjunction with a conference presented in October 1985 at Duke University on "New Developments in Health Law Databases." It is reprinted in the Appendix by permission of the Duke University Press, *Journal of Health Politics, Policy and Law*, where it was published in the Spring of 1986.

The above is an example of a service that many law libraries might consider providing. A request from a health law teacher to a local law library might induce the librarian to prepare and update a health law bibliography of local holdings that could be very helpful in preparing courses.

In addition, there are various other health law bibliographies that can be consulted for other selected listings, including these: *Law, Medicine & Health Care*, Reference List, monthly; *American Journal of Law & Medicine*, quarterly; *Legal Reference Services Quarterly*, Vol. 3(3), Fall 1983, *Law, Medicine and Health Care: A Bibliography*, James T. Ziegenfuss, Jr., New York: Facts on File Publications, 1984, 265 pp.; and *Ethics in Nursing*, (a bibliography), Terry Pence, New York: National League for Nursing, 1983, 147 pp.

CHAPTER 7

DEALING WITH LAWYERS IN A HEALTH CARE SETTING

MAKING THE LAWYER-CLIENT RELATIONSHIP WORK

One principle with which most observers of the American health industry agree is that the law continues to play an ever-increasing role in health care matters. The expanding scope and increasing complexity of governmental involvement in health care (including massive governmental purchases of health services), rapidly escalating competition for reduced financial resources, and conflicts caused by the increasing sophistication and risk of medical care have all contributed to the growing prominence of legal issues in health care. Understanding how to relate to and deal with lawyers is therefore of critical importance to the health administrator. In this chapter the lawyer-health care client relationship and its implications for the position of law in the health administration curriculum are discussed.

Comprehending the lawyer's role in relation to health care administration can produce undeniable benefits from a variety of perspectives: increased awareness of potential legal issues; earlier and more effective involvement of lawyers when they are needed; reduction of costs related to the use of lawyers; and, ultimately, diminished legal risks to the health care enterprise. It is self-evident that anyone training in health administration should understand both the proper relationship between lawyers and health care administrators and the efficient and effective use of lawyers.

The Role Of The Lawyer

An informed appreciation of the lawyer's relationship to the health care administrator begins with an understanding of the lawyer's skills and the types of matters in which these skills are relevant.

Identification, analysis, and resolution of issues

A lawyer's main task is to identify legal issues and apply legal principles to specific facts, circumstances, or transactions. At its most basic level, the required substantive analysis is purely syllogistic and deductive: general rules are applied to specific facts, and a specific conclusion is derived about the legal effects of these facts.

From the narrowly circumscribed area of technical legal analysis, which is the foundation of legal competence, the skillful lawyer is also able to identify and project the practical implications of proposed actions and responses. If the client requests, or if the lawyer deems it appropriate, the counselor's substantive legal analysis may be supplemented by review of and advice on a wide variety of nonlegal implications of a prior or proposed course of conduct, including its financial, practical, managerial, political, and human consequences. In many cases, proper identification and weighing of such tangential issues may be of more importance to a successful outcome than the purely legal matters.

Finally, the lawyer's technical and practical analysis may be translated into advice concerning the effects of proposed transactions. Advice may range from the formal opinion letter to the less formal reasoned opinion to the informal letter or memorandum of advice.

In understanding a lawyer's role in identifying and analyzing issues and in providing advice on such issues, the health care client should be aware of several underlying factors. First, while a lawyer can "find" the law on his own, the quality of his analysis and advice depends largely on the validity and reliability of the facts with which he is presented, whether actual or hypothetical. In many cases, those facts are within the purview of the client. Accordingly, the quality of the lawyer's work identification, analysis, and resolution of issues frequently depends on the client's ability to provide accurate and relevant factual information. To the extent that the client can do this without substantial prompting and guidance by the lawyer, significant savings in legal fees can be realized.

Second, clients have a misguided tendency to treat a lawyer's analysis as absolute and correct. In fact, how much weight should be given to legal analysis and advice may depend on several variables. For one thing, the health care administrator should realize that a lawyer is not under an absolute legal duty to provide the "correct" answer, but merely analysis and advice that is consistent with professional standards of knowledge, skill, and diligence. Thus, an incorrect analysis or answer may not be a violation of the lawyer's professional responsibility to the client, particularly in an uncertain or emerging area of the law. For another, the validity and reliability of a lawyer's judgment may be affected by several factors such as prior experience in similar matters, substantive expertise, knowledge of the health care client and its objectives, and familiarity with other participants in the matter under consideration.

Finally, a client may impose limitations on the lawyer by the nature of the advice or product it requests. For example, a request for a formal opinion letter generally will cause a lawyer to define the area of proposed analysis as narrowly as possible and to seek absolute certainty concerning the conclusion that is expressed. By contrast, a request for informal advice or analysis may result in a product that is more comprehensive, less conditional, and, ultimately, more useful to the client.

In any case, the health care administrator should recognize that identification and analysis of issues is the starting point at which every lawyer will begin every legal task, whether formally or informally. Understanding that process and the variables that accompanying it may dictate the utility and cost of the final product to the client.

Representation in formal legal proceedings

From the baseline of substantive legal analysis, which involves only the lawyer and the client, the appropriate use of the lawyer expands to third-party proceedings--formal and informal, adversarial, advisory, and friendly.

The most commonly recognized application of the lawyer's skills is formal litigation in court. A client can generally represent himself in judicial proceedings, but the presence of a lawyer at all stages is a virtual precondition to success. Even lawyers are ill-advised, despite their technical expertise, to represent themselves in legal matters--hence the quip "the lawyer who represents himself has a fool for a client."

In passing, all health care clients should be aware of the existence of a bifurcated court system in the United States. The federal court system deals with constitutional issues, "diversity" cases (i.e., disputes between citizens of different states), and matters arising under federal statutes such as antitrust actions, suits involving Medicare and other federal health programs, actions under the National Labor Relations Act, some health planning matters, and a host of other tax issues relevant to health care administrators. All other matters fall under the jurisdiction of the court systems of the individual states. These range from personal injury suits to appeals of state administrative agency actions and from contractual disputes to zoning issues.

Almost every health care client recognizes and accepts the necessity to be represented by a lawyer at all stages of formal litigation including initiation of suit, discovery proceedings, and court appearances. However, many health care enterprises have not fully recognized the significance of certain other types of formal and informal proceedings that occur outside the court system but that may have legal effects at least as significant as those created by a lawsuit. These proceedings tend to take four forms: three of those involve governmental administrative agencies; and the fourth involves private entities alone. The appropriate use of legal counsel in all these situations is of great importance to the health care institution.

One category of administrative agency proceeding, conducted by both federal and state governments, is the formal, quasi-judicial proceeding that is similar, in many respects, to a lawsuit. This category generally involves adversary hearings with formal records and procedures and generally may be followed by an appeal to a specified court. A wide range of health care matters can involve such proceedings, including certificate-of-need appeals, Medicare and Medicaid reimbursement and benefit determinations, zoning and property tax issues, and employment discrimination complaints.

A second category of administrative agency proceeding is the formal advisory proceeding characteristic of some federal and state agencies. Such proceedings allow private parties to secure formal advice from administrative agencies upon written request. Proceedings generally entail detailed procedures regarding the form and legal effects of such requests and the potential consequences of certain determinations or failures to respond on the part of the requesting party. Such types of actions include, for example, requests for private letter rulings from the Internal Revenue Service, determinations of nonreviewability under state certificate-of-need laws, and "no-action" letters from the Securities and Exchange Commission.

A third type of formal action before governmental administrative agencies involves administrative filings. These are exceptionally numerous in the health care field at both the federal and state levels and can include licensing applications, third-party payment claims, certificate-of-need applications, and other submissions related to regulatory requirements. The types of filings are too diverse to permit any generalization, other than to note that health care administrators are not aware of the need for many such filings, their effects are often not fully understood, and the consequences of failing to file properly and in a timely fashion may be significant.

A distinguishable category of governmental administrative proceeding is the informal proceeding, whereby the governmental agency may provide written or oral interpretation of regulations or policies, agree to meetings, or negotiate certain actions with regard to a potential area of its jurisdiction. While not conducted according to formal rules, the resolution of such matters may be based entirely on legal principles and may have formal and informal precedental effects of prior actions by a health care enterprise.

A final area in which clients (and lawyers) increasingly find themselves involved are formal proceedings in private venues. These matters can include proceedings internal to the health care enterprise, such as medical staff disciplinary hearings, employee grievances, and hearings conducted by the institution's governing board. Formal proceedings involving health care institutions and external parties have also proliferated, including such matters as arbitration of coverage and quality-of-care claims and third-party payment hearings (e.g., and third-party payment forums, e.g., Blue Cross).

Several points should be understood by any health care administrator faced with a formal adversarial proceeding, whether judicial, administrative, or private. (The same rules apply generally to filings and informal administrative agency actions.) First, the more formal the rules of the proceeding, the more a lawyer's help is likely to be useful. Second, formal or informal administrative proceedings can often foreclose other options, either legally or practically, and may have an adverse precedental effect. For example, many hospitals do not understand that their arguments are limited to the material contained in a certificate-of-need application and hearing if a later appeal is made to a state court. Third, administrative agency staff are sometimes as uncertain of the legal procedure and substance applicable to an administrative proceeding as the health care institution; thus, securing sound legal advice may help to relieve the confusion of either or both parties. On the other hand, it should be noted that a lawyer's involvement will sometimes eliminate the possibility of informal resolution of a matter by magnifying the seriousness of an issue, heightening the formality surrounding it, and raising the concerns of the other party. Good lawyers can often sense when this might be the case and suggest several ways in which their involvement can be more subtly handled.

Negotiation, identification, and resolution of issues in informal settings

A major area of legal involvement includes representation of health care clients in informal settings, including contractual negotiations, definition of internal policies and procedures, and formalization of internal arrangements for the health care institution.

The potential ways in which a lawyer may be involved are so varied as to defy tight definition, but generally they include identifying and framing the issues, gathering the pertinent facts, analyzing the client's objectives, advising the client internally or representing it in discussions with other parties, preparing position statements, communicating in writing formally and informally with other parties and with the client, and participating in meetings and formal or informal discussions. Lawyers might also include formal document resolutions to issues (e.g., by preparing transactional agreements such as contracts, leases, or financing documents); confirm terms of resolution with third parties (e.g., through formal and informal settlement documents and memoranda of understandings); and draft documents to memorialize internal actions by a health care institution (e.g., by preparing corporate articles and bylaws, medical staff bylaws, policies and procedures, and related matters).

Some points should be noted in regard to these functions. First, the degree of the lawyer's involvement in informal, nonadversarial matters is a function of several factors: the client's awareness of the potential legal issues involved, the client's prior experience with the lawyer in similar or related transactions, and the client's concern about external verification of preliminary conclusions. Second, as in the area of analysis and advice, the lawyer's ability to represent the client successfully and efficiently and to produce a responsive legal product is necessarily a function of the client's ability to identify facts, define desired results, and specify the scope of legal and nonlegal analysis expected of the lawyer. The client must realize that the lawyer's work product depends on the various elements provided by the client.

Client educational functions

The role of a lawyer in educating clients in legal and regulatory issues concerning health care matters has taken on special significance over the last decade. This is understandable in light of the rapidly increasing complexity of such issues and the fact that many directors of health care institutions are volunteers whose regular line of business is unrelated to the health care enterprise.

Such educational functions can take the form of written or oral presentations to management staff and/or the board. Topics for review by legal counsel tend to include the applicability of general principles of law in the health care environment (e.g., the use of general negligence rules in specialized malpractice cases), recent specialized developments in health care law and regulation, and case studies or models reflecting experiences and lessons derived from past similar situations. It should be noted that the appropriate lawyer to involve in this type of educational program varies from subject to subject. Indeed, it makes little sense for a lawyer who specializes in health care personal injury matters to discuss issues surrounding a highly specialized financial transaction or a collective bargaining agreement. To some, this observation will seem too obvious to bear statement; but clearly there are clients who expect their lawyers to be expert in all areas, and there are lawyers who, seeking to satisfy such expectations, will hold themselves out as possessing infinite expertise. This is not only inefficient, but it can also lead to serious problems when key decisions are mishandled.

General Counsel

In some cases, the lawyer's role extends far beyond the formal lawyer-client relationship, into general counseling on various aspects of the health care institution's business. These situations tend to arise in circumstances where a lawyer has extensive knowledge of and experience with a particular client, a close personal relationship with its senior management staff or director, or extensive specialized substantive expertise in similar transactions. Results of such counseling tend to be somewhat informal and frequently precede more formal involvement by the lawyer at a subsequent stage of the transaction, such as preparation of contracts or representation in litigation.

In some cases, a client may value the lawyer's business acumen or general ability to assimilate and organize information, identify issues and options, and assist in analysis of the practical costs and benefits of a course of action. The wisdom of relying on an attorney's general business advice may depend on several factors, including the lawyer's knowledge of and prior experience with similar matters, his understanding of the industry and client, his ability to identify and separate legal from nonlegal implications, and the institution's clear understanding of the benefits and limitations of his advice concerning nonlegal issues and judgments.

USING LAWYERS EFFECTIVELY

Once the potential role of legal counsel is understood, the health care client can begin to develop a checklist for dealing effectively with lawyers. Each client differs in its style and degree of comfort in dealing with attorneys. However, many seasoned health administrators agree that some or all of the following skills are helpful in making effective use of lawyers.

Sensitivity to potential legal implications

This factor depends entirely on the client's understanding of the substantive and procedural rules that may come into play in a specific matter. The client who understands possible legal implications can determine at an early date whether to involve a lawyer. Additionally, sensitivity to legal issues may assist in eliminating unproductive options and in avoiding actions or statements that may damage or prejudice the client's interests at a later date. The very best of lawyers cannot change events once they have occurred or alter statements once they have been made. Many worthwhile cases have been lost because of failure to appreciate legal nuances at an early stage.

Early involvement of the lawyer where needed

If a client is going to involve a lawyer in a transaction, it is generally preferable to do so at the earliest feasible stage. This allows the lawyer to practice "preventive law," producing a "clean record" and thereby avoiding subsequent legal problems, clarifying relevant facts and objectives, and avoiding duplication of effort and potential pitfalls. Early involvement of counsel can also aid the client in understanding its legal options and the legal and nonlegal implications of various courses of action. Finally, involving a lawyer early on may actually save the client money. Any experienced lawyer can point to transactions where delayed legal involvement resulted in the time-consuming and expensive necessity to undo a transaction and start over.

Assembly and disclosure of relevant information

Before involving a lawyer, the client should identify the initial facts and objectives that it believes are relevant. Doing so will help to define the context of the matter and the desired result and direct the lawyer in his legal evaluations. Of course, relevant facts and objectives may change as transactions proceed, and the lawyer's judgment about what is relevant may differ from that of the client. However, the initial effort to collect this basic information generally will lead to increased efficiency and responsiveness on the part of the lawyer.

There is also a need for full disclosure on the part of the client to the lawyer. The lawyer should be apprised of all relevant information, even if it is potentially harmful or embarrassing to the client. Clients are surprisingly reluctant to reveal essential information to their lawyers when it reveals a lapse or failing on the client's part. Clients should understand that most communications between client and lawyer are confidential and subject to a privilege against compelled disclosure. Equally as important, a client should understand that full disclosure of all facts and circumstances is a practical necessity if the lawyer is to engage effectively in legal reasoning, which involves matching the facts to the law and formulating conclusions and recommendations.

Definition of the lawyer's role

Too often, clients believe that the lawyer's role is absolutely clear: provide legal advice. While that may sound simple, its implementation is a far more difficult and complex task. To ensure effective use of a lawyer, a client should identify the proposed objectives of the lawyer's involvement, the expected timetable, and the nature of the expected legal product. Ideally, all these elements should be clarified at or near the beginning of the lawyer's involvement.

One fact that clients seem to find particularly hard to accept is that the law is very rarely clear or absolute. Despite the tremendous volume of case and statutory law that exists, a large proportion of the questions and problems that arise in legal matters have no direct precedent or legislative pronouncement from which a simple answer can be gleaned. The lawyer's role, then, is often to reason by analogy, taking what is known and using it to predict how courts, administrative agencies, and the like, will react. Clients tend to expect that the law contains "the answer" and that the lawyer, with a bit of library research, can ascertain it. Much more likely, however, is that the lawyer will present the results of his inquiry in the form of a range of options, each with one or more likely scenarios flowing from it. These will be handed back to the client with whatever information is available to enable the client to make a decision. Some clients may consider this the lawyer's way of "passing the buck," but in many cases it is the only sound and professional thing for the lawyer to do.

Sometimes, clients--and especially health care clients, it seems--are reluctant to ask for written confirmation of legal analysis and conclusions. In many cases, however, written confirmation of facts and analysis is the most cost-effective way to ensure that the client and the lawyer understand one another and that relevant facts have been identified accurately. Any such document should include an explanation of the law in terms that are understandable to the client and an identification of the analysis involved, including the options considered. Written analysis can be crucial to avoiding misunderstandings and memorializing the client's consideration of an issue, which can, in turn, prevent future legal problems. Clients, anxious to keep legal fees to a minimum, may ask for an oral statement of the lawyer's conclusions. In matters of significant complexity, this may prove a false economy.

Response to the lawyer's recommendation

Once a lawyer has been hired, the health care client should expect to respond to the analysis and recommendations the lawyer presents. At the very least, it should review the lawyer's recommendations and understand the underlying principles and reasoning and their applicability to the problem. Moreover, the client probably should presume that the lawyer's advice will be followed except where it is clearly inappropriate to do so and where good reasons for not doing so are fully identified. If a lawyer is competent to render a determination, his expertise and the expense to the client of retaining his services justify a presumption that his recommendation should be followed. Furthermore, in dismissing recommendations cavalierly or without adequate understanding, the client may not appreciate all the legal and practical consequences of failure to follow those recommendations and may incur undue risk. Thus, the client should be prepared to follow formal procedures in modifying or rejecting legal advice. Reasons for such actions should be identified, or should potentially identify useful modifications to the advice. Finally, the client's conclusion should be communicated to the lawyer.

Definition of administrative and financial arrangements

Clear, early definition of administrative and financial arrangements with lawyers is perhaps the single most overlooked area of client-lawyer relations, although recent trends appear to be changing this historical oversight.

At the outset of a relationship, clients and lawyers should agree on administrative responsibilities. The lawyer should identify the persons primarily and secondarily responsible for contact in his office and any other lawyers involved in a specific matter. The client should designate one or more persons to coordinate contacts with the lawyer and should identify persons to be contacted within the client's office. The client and lawyer should agree to timetables, responsibilities for fact gathering, and the nature of the final product.

Perhaps most important, the client and lawyer should discuss and understand the economic arrangements for the lawyer's services. The client should understand the general types of fee arrangements applicable to the lawyer's services (i.e., hourly billing, contingency fees, guaranteed rate for project, or retainer arrangements) and the lawyer's billing policies for the matter. Fees should be discussed at the outset of the relationship. And where appropriate, a client should ask for an estimate at this time, recognizing, however, that projecting an exact cost in advance may not be feasible. Finally, the lawyer should inform the client of proposed billing arrangements, including the frequency of billing, and the detail and documentation that will be contained in the billing.

Understanding the lawyer's objectives

A key consideration in successful lawyer-client relationships is the client's ability to understand the lawyer's objectives. Most attorneys want to provide their clients with a successful outcome consistent with the law. They also want to help their clients avoid future legal problems while conforming to professional standards of responsibility and behavior. This last point may lead to significant tensions when the lawyer encounters some practice, or proposed practice, of the client with which he is very uncomfortable. The client may have been doing certain things improperly for some time--e.g., failing to follow certain legally required procedures--but not yet encountered any problems. The lawyer, once aware of this practice, may view much more seriously the risk involved in the client's continuing to proceed in the same way. In essence, the lawyer unearths a problem the client did not know it had and then must press for its correction, even though this may pose a considerable present cost. The client may prefer to save that cost, and risk instead the greater future cost if the improper procedure is detected. The lawyer, though, is held to the higher standards of conduct that his better knowledge of the area and his professional principles would support. Skillful lawyers, in most cases, can persuade the increased present cost, but this is the type of situation that can provoke tensions and dissatisfaction on the part of the client.

Avoidance of common pitfalls

A frequent problem in lawyer-client relationships is that the client fails to understand the limitations inherent in the lawyer's role and is thus dissatisfied or disappointed with the lawyer's work product. Among the more common of these misunderstandings are the following:

1. The client expects a lawyer to reach an action decision, which is ultimately the client's responsibility, rather than render advice or recommendations.

2. The client treats the lawyer's advice as absolute and immutable without considering the law's lack of clarity on many points or changed facts or objectives.

3. The client expects counsel to take into account initial or changed facts, circumstances, or objectives that have not been disclosed by the client to the lawyer.

4. The client holds the lawyer responsible for correct legal conclusions and recommendations that are inconsistent with the client's desired result or with the client's view of the ideal law (commonly referred to as "killing the messenger").

5. The client blames the lawyer for delays, inefficiencies, or unexpected costs where the client has failed to disclose information, failed to define administrative arrangements, modified timetables or expected products, changed transactions in midstream, or failed to define expectation clearly.

6. The client leaves it to counsel to organize all relevant factual materials, rather than providing him with as much information as it is able to compile.

7. The client engages the lawyer in unnecessarily long conversations, mindless of the fact that the "meter is running," and then is later annoyed at the amount of time consumed by the project.

THE ROLE OF INSIDE COUNSEL

In the health care industry, as in other businesses, recent years have seen a rapid expansion in the use of inside counsel to fill many roles traditionally served by outside lawyers. This trend can be expected to continue. However, the effective use of in-house counsel requires an appreciation and understanding on the part of the health care administrator of several areas that frequently are not defined clearly.

Basic functions

When an inside lawyer is employed as a regular member of the management staff, he obviously should be able to fulfill (or at least arrange for the fulfillment of) the required legal functions. However, it should be recognized that inside counsel, as a member of the management and administrative staff, has a role that should be more expansive than that of an outside lawyer who is not involved in day-to-day administration.

The management functions of inside counsel can, and generally do, include some or all of the following: adding a legal component to basic management decisions; formulating policies and procedures; designing internal monitoring systems; coordinating legal information provided in management decisions; educating management and the board; handling routine legal matters, such as contracts, minutes, and resolutions; and coordinating relationships with outside legal counsel. Careful consideration should be given to these various functions when the inside counsel first comes on board and an early attempt made to define the priorities of these respective roles, with particular regard for effective use of the attorney's time.

Appropriate use of outside counsel

A common misconception on the part of health care administrators is the belief that retention of inside counsel will eliminate or reduce significantly the necessity to use outside counsel. This assumption frequently is incorrect for various reasons, including the fact that the inside counsel is likely to identify more issues that require complicated or objective judgments on the part of outside counsel.

When inside counsel is hired, management staff and the board should attempt to define those generic circumstances in which use of outside counsel may be considered. One obvious occasion would be when independent legal opinion is required as a matter of business practice or law, such as in a financing or an area involving conflicts of interest. Another occasion would be to handle specialized issues arising on a one-time or infrequent basis and therefore not warranting the time it would take to educate inside counsel in specialty areas. Such matters can include securities, tax, and antitrust matters. A third type of issue that may justify the retention of outside counsel is an unusually complicated or time-consuming administrative or judicial proceeding that would overburden inside counsel, such as a major antitrust case, practice litigation, or hearings under the National Labor Relations Act. A fourth and related type of issue is one in which prior experience or knowledge of a particular forum, including an administrative agency or court, is important. Such cases can include reimbursement, patent, tax, and complicated local or state administrative issues.

Several points should be emphasized. First, hiring inside counsel will not eliminate the need for outside counsel. Second, some effort should be made to define in advance cases where use of outside counsel may be appropriate. Third, inside counsel should be intimately involved in both the initial evaluation of types of cases and particular cases where outside counsel may be retained and in the coordination of internal and external legal efforts on behalf of the health enterprise.

Common mistakes made in using inside counsel

The recent increase in the use of inside counsel in the health industry has led to mistakes that are common during the initial stages of any evolving business practice. A clear understanding of problem areas will enhance the effectiveness of inside counsel and maximize his benefit to the organization. Common mistakes and misconceptions include the following:

1. Failure to include inside counsel at the earliest stage possible--strategic and business planning--with resultant loss of legal input;

2. Overcommitment of inside counsel to routine day-to-day matters, with loss of legal perspective and potential increased reliance on outside counsel;

3. Failure to define generic circumstances where use of outside counsel may be appropriate;

4. Exclusion of inside counsel from the process of selecting and coordinating with outside counsel;

5. Underestimation of the economic benefits of "preventive law" practice by inside counsel and the resultant benefits flowing from potential expansion of size of inside counsel's staff.

TEACHING PROSPECTIVE HEALTH ADMINISTRATORS HOW TO WORK WITH LAWYERS

For a faculty member wishing to teach students of health administration to work effectively with lawyers, simply being aware of the various points raised above is an important first step. Health law teachers who are also legal practitioners are more likely to be sensitive to these issues than are full-time academics, but even working on a regular basis with health administrators does not guarantee that one will fully comprehend the dynamics of the interaction between the manager and the lawyer. One must therefore begin by considering carefully the specific knowledge and skills that students must acquire to be effective in this endeavor. Then follows the challenging task of deciding how to convey the appropriate mix of elements to them.

Obviously, this is not simply a matter of having students read the first part of this chapter. Some of the information can be fully understood only in an operational context; students must observe certain principles in actual practice to appreciate them properly. The problem is further compounded by the myriad different operational styles favored by health care institutions, administrators, and lawyers. There simply is no single right way to relate to lawyers; it is a matter of individual discretion and judgment, attributes that some would contend cannot be taught in the classroom at all, but must, instead, be learned in the "real world."

Nonetheless, it is possible to bring a bit of the "real world" into the classroom or, conversely, to extend the classroom beyond its conventional boundaries. Giving students a chance and a reason to think about how they will deal with lawyers when they encounter them on the job may make a worthwhile difference in how they will actually perform when the time comes. There are a number of approaches that can be used, either singly or in combination, in a health law course to provide students with the opportunity and the motivation for learning this important operational skill.

THE VALUE OF TEACHING LEGAL FUNDAMENTALS

Providing students with even a basic knowledge of the legal system and the legal aspects of health care can affect very positively the way they subsequently interact with lawyers. In any profession, the rapport between the professional and the client is enhanced when the client better understands the professional's field and appreciates the complexity and subtlety of the professional's role. Familiarity with basic terminology and concepts of the field can also be useful, facilitating communication and removing some of the "black box" intimidation of an unknown technical area.

Most of us have heard it said (some of us may have even said it ourselves) that a lawyer will treat a client with more respect when he perceives that the client knows something about the substantive matter in question. Whether one accepts this assertion or not, it seems logical that there are at least three positive effects of giving students a solid, albeit fundamental, grounding in law. First, one who understands something of the law is better able to spot the legal issues in situations that arise and, thus, will know better when to call for the lawyer's assistance--hopefully before problems become too severe or situations too inflexibly defined. Timing of the legal intervention, as indicated earlier, can make a crucial difference. Second, a legally sophisticated health care administrator will probably know better how to frame an issue and present it to a lawyer, along with necessary supporting information, in a way that enables him to deal with it efficiently. Turning a matter over to one's counsel in a complete, logical, and organized form saves the lawyer time and the client money. Third, one who knows something about how the law is structured and how it works will, presumably, have greater sympathy for the difficulties the lawyer may face in giving a straightforward, unambiguous answer to problems that arise in the client's work situation. This last point addresses a commonly heard complaint about lawyers: that they rarely, if ever, seem able to give a simple answer to a simple question. Clients who understand why this is so will find it easier to accept and work with the lawyer's work product.

POSSIBLE TEACHING APPROACHES

An informal survey of faculty who are teaching health law courses reveals that few of them make a special point of teaching client-lawyer interactional skills. It is generally easier and less time-consuming to convey substantive information than to try to create or hone operational abilities. Therefore, given the time and resource constraints under which most health law courses are taught, many instructors opt to teach substantive law and hope for the best in terms of the students' using the information to improve their future relationships with lawyers. Still, there are numerous techniques that can be used to lead students to a greater understanding of client-lawyer relationships and even to give them actual practice in making such relationships more effective. The following subsections cover numerous techniques that have been tried in various courses. Teachers are encouraged to experiment with some of these approaches, or variants thereof, and to devise other mechanisms appropriate to their own individual program settings.

Research projects

Students may be assigned research projects on practical, real-life questions that will cause them to seek out and consult local attorneys for help in defining and resolving the issues. Obviously, such a technique requires assembling a panel of local attorneys who have expressed a willingness to be consulted on this basis. Since "a lawyer's time is his stock in trade" (a quote attributed to Abraham Lincoln), the faculty member must take care to ensure that students understand the value of this resource and use it wisely. It is also important that both students and attorney-volunteers understand the rules of the game and share roughly equal expectations of what each will contribute and get out of such interactions. Often the lawyer may see some benefit in having one or more students working on a research project that he has helped design. Thus, the teacher should take care to involve volunteers in the planning of the projects and should stay closely involved throughout the projects to make sure that they are of maximum possible benefit and satisfaction to both the attorneys and the students. Volunteers should, in most if not all cases, be given the chance to see the student's work product.

Independent studies

Closely related to the concept of a research project is that of an independent study project that a student can work on with a practicing attorney. This is most likely to be successful when the attorney has a case or project on which he is working and the faculty member can supervise the exercise adequately to ensure its academic utility. Health administration students can work with a tutor or preceptor at a law firm or the legal department of a health institution, state government agency, or other similar setting on a research project of relevance to their special interests. Typically, such projects involve both legal and nonlegal elements, and the student's help on the latter is the incentive for the participation of the outside party.

University rules applicable to such outside engagements must be observed; often there is a prohibition against students receiving financial compensation for projects done for academic course credit. There may also be issues of confidentiality to be considered. Finally, it must be decided how and to what extent the faculty member will involve the outside party in grading the student's work; a general delegation of grading authority will virtually never be acceptable. Such practical aspects should be discussed beforehand and all parties should be clear on the "ground rules" prior to initiation of the project.

Practitioner interviews

Another useful and interesting related type of exercise is to assign students to interview selected lawyers who are willing to take the time to discuss their roles as hospital counsel, insurance counsel, trial attorneys, and so on. The effectiveness of this mechanism can be enhanced by having the students report back to the class on the interviews. Of special interest might be reports on various fees and other compensation arrangements for the use of regular counsel, including contingency fee, salary, and various retainer arrangements.

Guest lectures

A common approach, and one that has a long tradition and is generally well received by students, is to invite practicing lawyers to class to discuss their health law practice activities in general or particular cases or transactions in which they have recently been involved with health service clients. This can work especially well if the guest is asked in advance to give some thought specifically to the question of how well the lawyer-client relationship worked in that particular situation and, if appropriate, how it could have been handled more effectively. Even if the practitioner's presentation is only a series of "war stories," so long as they are on point and well told they will be enjoyed by the students and will be of value. A variant of the single guest speaker approach that often works well is a session in which an institutional administrator and the institution's counsel come together and discuss the favorable and unfavorable (or the "best" and "worst") aspects of their working relationship. With some forethought and sensitivity, the faculty member can keep the interaction at a level sufficiently nonspecific to avoid having a "chilling effect" on the guest participants.

The problem with this suggestion is less likely to be in recruiting volunteer practitioners than in finding the time to indulge in what, admittedly, is often an inefficient educational exercise. Perhaps such presentations can best be handled outside of regular class time, in the form of "brown bag" discussions or late-afternoon, student-sponsored speaker series. As a regularly used teaching method, guest speakers often do not work well, especially if the faculty member has not taken care to integrate the guest's presentation with the specific needs of a particular part of the course. However, as an occasional "leaven," a guest speaker can be most effective.

One final point must be made. Guest speakers should not be used as substitutes for the teacher's own preparation. The faculty member must prepare both himself and the guest and should always attend at the guest's presentation. Not only is this an appropriate courtesy to the guest; it is necessary to maintain continuity in the course. Proper use of guest speakers can take as much or more preparation and management time than teaching a class oneself; faculty not prepared to make such a commitment of effort should not use this technique.

Related university courses

Students with an interest in understanding how lawyers function might be encouraged to take appropriate courses in other units of the university, such as the business school, to learn negotiating skills, or the law school, on any relevant subject.

Professional meetings

Students can be encouraged, or even financially assisted by the program, to attend professional meetings where lawyers are making health law presentations on current, relevant issues. Good examples of such activities are the American College of Healthcare Executives Congress and meetings of the local or state bar associations. Student rates for such meetings are regularly offered by many organizations, including the American Society of Law and Medicine and the National Health Lawyers Association.

Even where such discounts are not advertised, the faculty member may be able to negotiate such concessions on an ad hoc basis. As a motivational device, students can vie for the honor of being sent to selected professional meetings as the program's student representative.

INCENTIVES FOR PARTICIPATION BY PRACTITIONERS

The above ideas merely scratch the surface of the innovative approaches that can be used to give students the flavor of lawyer-client relations in the "real world." Whatever approaches are tried, however, will likely raise the question of what must be offered to obtain and maintain the involvement of persons outside the health administration program in these activities.

An attorney-volunteer's interest can vary tremendously from one setting to another. In some communities, the opportunity to be involved with an academic program at a respected institution is a sufficient attraction in itself. A term of acknowledgment used in course descriptions, syllabi, and the like, has appeal even though it is understood not to be a formal title granted by the university. "Teaching affiliate," "affiliated practitioner," and "preceptor" are descriptive terms that come readily to mind. Practitioners who participate on such a basis may be invited to health administration program activities such as colloquia and annual alumni day programs and given public recognition for their contributions. Of course, such opportunities for lawyers to interact with a particular program are more likely to be attractive to local lawyers if the students are graduate or postgraduate students who are currently or soon will be working in the field in that geographic area. But most lawyers are true believers in the long-term promotional benefits of community involvement; despite the immediate value of their contributed time, they often do not have to see an immediate return on their investment in order to be motivated to make it. Moreover, many legal practitioners will welcome the opportunity to try teaching or tutorial activities even when there is no likelihood of turning this to business advantage. Health law faculty, if they are actively involved in and known to the legal community, can readily tap this valuable resource for the benefit of their students.

CHAPTER 8

CONTINUING EDUCATION FOR HEALTH LAW TEACHERS

Interest in adult and continuing education has reached enormous levels in recent years. The National Advisory Council on Continuing Education has reported that over 23 million adults participate in continuing education annually. Continuing education is important and necessary for today's health care managers, health lawyers, and, especially, health law teachers, all of whom must stay abreast of a constantly changing body of health laws, regulations, and other literature. No longer can any professional rely upon the knowledge acquired in his or her initial educational program, expecting that such information will be sufficient for current day problems and situations. Activities to maintain knowledge and skill levels and resources from which to obtain currently needed information are essential to effectiveness in any professional field. With health care administrators becoming more aware of their legal responsibilities and potential liability for the actions of their institutions, their employees, and affiliated independent contractors, continuing education opportunities for health law teachers become even more important.

Health law represents a particularly difficult substantive area in which to keep current for three main reasons. First, the health care field has literally mushroomed over the past two decades, yielding an enormous quantity and variety of professional and trade literature in a multitude of subfields. Second, since Health Law interacts closely with so many related fields--health economics, labor and employee relations, organizational behavior, finance, medical technology, and information systems, to name just a few--a general familiarity with nonlegal developments in these areas is essential to a full understanding of the legal aspects. Finally, health law itself has been in a state of change throughout this period, with a proliferation of different state and federal statutory, regulatory, and case law developments and trends. The health law teacher must, therefore, be conversant with a vast body of knowledge and also have a highly developed array of legal bibliographic and research skills. Moreover, he or she must be able to impart some of those skills to future health care administrators.

Many who will use this Curriculum Guide will be in the process of expanding into health law from related fields of legal education or practice. Getting an initial grounding in this field and maintaining currency in it is a challenge of not insignificant proportions. This chapter seeks to help by presenting an overview of continuing education opportunities and information sources for health law teachers. The first section presents and briefly describes the major health law professional organizations, their principal activities, publications, and their membership structures and requirements. The second section discusses the availability of health law workshops, symposia, and conference opportunities. The third section presents a list of health law publications and information sources. A final section considers what role health law and health law teachers can and should play in promoting continuing education opportunities in health law for others. An appendix containing information on health law organizations, professional contacts, and literature sources is also included.

HEALTH LAW PROFESSIONAL ORGANIZATIONS

The task of becoming and staying knowledgeable in health law is aided by the large number of health law organizations around the United States. Counting just the principal organizations, without taking account of possible overlaps in membership, there are close to 20,000 persons involved in these organizations as of late 1986. As a group, these organizations are committed to stimulating and educating their members and to advancing knowledge and understanding of medical-legal issues. There are countless health law-related organizations with limited geographic and substantive focuses and relatively small memberships. This section will focus on the larger organizations, those with memberships in excess of 500 persons. All of these are nonprofit organizations with a nationwide membership. The five organizations, in alphabetical order, are the American Academy of Hospital Attorneys, the American Bar Association's Forum Committee on Health Law, the American College of Legal Medicine, the American Society of Law and Medicine, and the National Health Lawyers Association.

AMERICAN ACADEMY OF HOSPITAL ATTORNEYS (AAHA)

Focus and Membership

Based in Chicago, the American Association of Hospital Attorneys is affiliated with the American Hospital Association (AHA) and is oriented toward the interests of attorneys serving AHA member institutions. To join the AAHA, one must be admitted to the bar and be affiliated with a firm or organization eligible for AHA membership. Currently, the AAHA has approximately 3,000 attorney members. It was originally formed in 1967 under the name "American Society of Hospital Attorneys," but changed to its current name in 1983. The organization's professed goals are to provide members with the opportunity to meet and hear other attorneys who are expert in many areas of health law, to provide a source of professional reference to members, and to disseminate information on health care law and legislation and keep members abreast of notable court decisions. Because of the requirement that all members be attorneys in hospital-related practice, the AAHA has a narrower approach but covers the same broad range of substantive topics as the other organizations described herein.

Publications

The Academy has two regular publications and also publishes workbooks summarizing its annual institutes on Health Care Planning and Tax Law. These workbooks typically are sold for $95 each. Members of the Academy also receive

Health Law Vigil, a useful newsletter on current legal developments, published twice monthly by the American Hospital Association.

Hospital Law. The Academy's principal publication is its bimonthly newsletter on hospital law topics. *Hospital Law's* regular features include Labor Relations Report, Tax Quarterly, Coalitions Perspective, Malpractice Reports, and Washington Summary; in addition, there are various special reports. A subscription is $150 for AHA members, $200 for nonmembers.

The Hospital Medical Staff. This monthly newsletter is designed to inform and educate health care managers and lawyers on legal issues affecting hospital-medical staff relations. An annual subscription is $6.

Programs and Other Activities

AAHA sponsors approximately six 2-1/2 day educational programs annually on various legal topics of interest to health care practitioners and health lawyers, such as medical staff credentialing, health care risk management, hospital-physician joint ventures, and management of perinatal risks.

Membership Requirements, Types, and Fees

The Academy's members are divided into two categories, senior and affiliate. Senior membership is open to any lawyer serving a client eligible for membership in the American Hospital Association. This includes attorneys in law firms and those serving as in-house counsel to health care institutions. Senior members receive all of the AAHA's regular publications for an annual dues payment of $115. Additional attorneys meeting the requirements for senior membership can enroll as affiliate members at a reduced rate of $50 annually if their firm or organization has one senior member in good standing. Affiliate members receive only *Hospital Law*.

Contact

Ms. Shirley A. Worthy, Executive Director
American Academy of Hospital Attorneys
840 N. Lake Shore Drive
Chicago, IL 60611
Phone: (312) 280-6600

AMERICAN BAR ASSOCIATION (ABA), FORUM COMMITTEE ON HEALTH LAW

Focus and Membership

One of many specialty sections and committees of the ABA, the Forum Committee on health law concentrates on legal problems and interdependent relationships of providers and recipients of health care and the parties financially responsible for such matters. Its membership includes approximately 3,000 practicing lawyers and 1,000 law students. To belong, one must be a member of the ABA and one of its sections.

Publications

The Committee publishes a newsletter called *The Health Lawyer* which features reports of current events, short articles, and book reviews. It also issues an annual membership directory listing names and addresses, by state, of all members of the Forum Committee on Health Law. This directory facilitates communication among the members and is useful for lawyers and health care managers who need to know who to contact to gain information on specific health-related topics.

Programs and Activities

The Forum Committee on Health Law sponsors two or three educational programs each year on current topics.

A representative program is "Everything You Should Know about HMOs and PPOs," to be offered in 1987.

Membership Requirements, Types, and Fees

To join the Forum Committee on Health Law, one must belong to the ABA and also be a member of one of its specialty sections. Membership dues are $25, which does not include the charge for joining the ABA section, as required. All Forum Committee publicatons are included in the membership cost; other ABA publications, including the monthly ABA Journal, are included in the basic ABA and section membership. Student membership, at a fee of $5 per year, is open to members of the ABA's Law Students Division.

Contact

Ms. Carol S. Albrecht
Director of Forum Committees
American Bar Association
750 N. Lake Shore Drive
Chicago, IL 60611
Phone: (312) 988-5579

AMERICAN COLLEGE OF LEGAL MEDICINE (ACLM)

Focus and Membership

The central focus of this organization, which originated in 1955 and was officially incorporated in 1960, is forensic medicine. A unique aspect of the College is its membership, which is largely composed of professionals holding degrees in both medicine and law. In recent years, however, the membership of close to 1,000 persons has been broadened by the inclusion of a growing number of Associates in law, medicine, or science who hold a single professional degree relevant to the field of legal medicine. Associates participate fully in the College's activities, but to become a Fellow of the College of Legal Medicine (FCLM), one must have dual degrees in law and medicine.

The ACLM's stated purpose is to unite those who are engaged in the practice of, or otherwise especially interested in, legal medicine; to encourage specialization in this field; to elevate standards of the field by fostering and encouraging study and research; to elevate standards of postgraduate education for qualification as a specialist in this area; to conduct professional and educational meetings; and to edit and publish books, journals, and other educational materials in this and related fields. Starting from its central interest in forensic medicine, the College has broadened its focus over the years to include the full range of topics in legal medicine and health law generally.

Publications

The College publishes two journals and a periodic newsletter, which reports College-related events and information to its members.

Journal of Legal Medicine. This scholarly journal, of law-review format, is published quarterly. It features lead articles by academics and practitioners in legal medicine and related fields, student comments, generally authored by students at the Southern Illinois University School of Law, with which the Journal is affiliated, and in-depth review essays of important new books in the field of legal medicine. Other features, such as focused symposia on current topics, e.g., medical malpractice, are sometimes included. A subscription to the Journal, which is included in the ACLM membership fee, is $56 annually if purchased separately.

Legal Aspects of Medical Practice. A monthly, magazine-format journal, LAMP, as it is called, features short articles, reports of case decisions, book reviews, reports of current events, etc. A subscription, if purchased separate from membership in the College, is $56 annually.

Programs and Activities

In the spring of each year, the College holds its International Conference on Legal Medicine; the 27th annual conference will be held in May 1987 in Long Beach, California. These conferences are highly structured and content-packed 3-1/2 day academic programs at which a large number of scholarly papers are presented. Proceedings are generally published. Other shorter programs are held throughout the year on an ad hoc basis, sometimes in conjunction with other organizations. A regular one-day meeting on legal medicine topics is held each fall.

Membership Requirements, Types, and Fees

To become a member, one must hold a degree in law, medicine, or a health-related science and must be sponsored by a current ACLM member. Full recognition as a Fellow of the College is limited to persons with degrees in both law and medicine. Associate memberships are open to those with a degree in law, medicine, or science, and Affiliate memberships are available to persons with a degree in either law or medicine who are pursuing a degree in the other field. In 1986, the annual membership fee was $115, which includes all publications.

Contact

Mr. Thomas W. Teal, Executive Secretary
American College of Legal Medicine
858 Welsh Road, Suite 9
Maple Glen, PA 19002
Phone: (215) 646-6800

AMERICAN SOCIETY OF LAW AND MEDICINE (ASLM)

Focus and Membership

The Boston-based American Society of Law and Medicine was founded in 1972 "to provide a forum for interdisciplinary discussion of the complex issues at the interface of law, medicine and health care." The largest of the health law organizations, ASLM has the most diverse membership. While more than half of its approximately 6,000 members hold degrees in law, ASLM's membership also includes health care administrators, physicians, nurses, allied health professionals, academics in health-related fields, and students of various types. Reflecting the breadth of its membership, the Society brings an interdisciplinary approach to its exploration of issues in law and medicine and puts special emphasis on promoting understanding among different types of professionals working in the health care field.

ASLM has traditionally had somewhat of a patients' rights, bioethics, and humanist focus, as evidenced mainly in the subject matter of its educational programs and its publications; but in recent years, reflecting trends in the health care system generally, it has increasingly paid attention to issues of health systems organization, reimbursement, antitrust, and other more business-oriented aspects of health care delivery.

A worthwhile adjunct to ASLM's OTHER activities is the maintenance of the Sagall Library of Law, Medicine & Health Care, which is located at the Society's headquarters in the building which houses the Boston University School of Law. Membership in the Society includes library privileges.

For health law teachers, a most important aspect of ASLM's activities is its support of a Health Law Teacher's Section to serve as a forum for teachers of health law in graduate and professional schools of law, medicine, public health, dental medicine, nursing, and health administration. Reduced ASLM membership rates are offered to full-time health law teachers, and the Section holds an annual meeting to share substantive knowledge about health law topics and ideas for teaching in these areas. These meetings are structured to be especially helpful to newcomers to the field of health law teaching.

In 1983, the Society established a Task Force on Health Law Curricula, chaired by Professor Wendy K. Mariner of Harvard University, and charged to (1) develop an overview of the health law field; (2) describe the objectives and benefits of teaching health law in different types of schools; (3) provide examples of health law courses for different types of schools; and (4) make recommendations for health law curriculum content in different types of schools. The activities of this Task Force were related to and synergistic with those of our current AUPHA Task Force; and the two bodies, which had a liaison through Professor David G. Warren, coordinated their efforts and shared information in their pursuit of common goals. In 1985, the ASLM group published its report, HEALTH LAW AND PROFESSIONAL EDUCATION. This document, which should be most helpful to health law teachers and directors of health administration programs, is available through ASLM.

The Society publishes two quarterly journals, described below. It also occasionally publishes books of essays on selected health law topics. Two examples are LEGAL AND ETHICAL ASPECTS OF HEALTH CARE FOR THE ELDERLY (M.B. Kapp, H.E. Pies, and A.E. Doudera, eds., 1986) and INSTITUTIONAL ETHICS COMMITTEES AND HEALTH CARE DECISION MAKING (R.E. Cranford and A.E. Doudera, eds., 1984).

American Journal of Law and Medicine (AJLM). This scholarly journal of the law review format is co-published quarterly with the Boston University School of Law. In addition to articles on medical-legal issues, it contains two regular features summarizing significant new information in the field: Selected Recent Court Decisions and Selected Book Releases. If purchased separately, a subscription to this journal costs $48 per year; subscription is included in ASLM membership.

Law, Medicine & Health Care (*LM&HC*). This journal, which is currently moving to a quarterly publication cycle, uses a magazine-style format and is, thus, less formal in appearance. In content and scholarly rigor, however, it is much like a law review, with articles that are strongly substantive and well documented. A useful feature of *LM&HC* is the Medicolegal Reference Shelf, which contains citations to court cases, periodical articles, books, pamphlets, and other materials catalogued in the Society's Sagall Library. Copies of most cited materials can be obtained through the library's photocopy service. *LM&HC* also contains book reviews, "Health Care Briefs," which are synopses of newsworthy events in health law, and a registry of upcoming meetings.

Subscription to *LM&HC*, included in ASLM membership, costs $40 annually if purchased separately.

Programs and Activities

ASLM sponsors about 12 programs per year--called "Critical Issues in Health Law"--that focus either on particular topics or cover a broad range of currently noteworthy subjects These programs, which generally run two days in length, are offered in various locations around the country, and occasionally overseas, at relatively modest charges. As noted above, an annual meeting is held specifically for health law teachers. This Health Law Teachers Conference is held on different university campuses, including the Society's home campus of Boston University, on a rotating basis. The conference usually runs for 2-1/2 days and features sessions devoted to substantive topics in health law and others dealing with pedagogic techniques. Breakout sessions allow part of the conference to be tailored to the needs and interests of specific types of schools, and the conference is usually balanced between its attention to new health law faculty and "veterans."

Membership Requirements, Types, and Fees

Regular membership is open to any attorney, hospital or nursing home administrator, physician, nurse, academic professional, or allied health professional. The annual membership fee includes subscriptions to the Society's two journals and privileges at the Sagall Library of Law, Medicine and Health Care. A discount book purchase service and an option to enroll in the Society's group life insurance plan are also included. Annual dues are $85 for regular members and $65 for fulltime health law teachers. A student membership, at an annual cost of $40, is offered to students enrolled fulltime in any of the areas listed in the regular membership categories.

Contact

Lawrence O. Gostin, Executive Director
American Society of Law and Medicine
765 Commonwealth Avenue - 16th Floor
Boston, Massachusetts   02215
Phone: (617) 262-4990

NATIONAL HEALTH LAWYERS ASSOCIATION (NHLA)

Focus and Membership

"Established in 1971 as a nonpartisan, nonpolitical body, the National Health Lawyers Association (NHLA) is a legal education society dedicated to the dissemination to members of timely and accurate information on the health field." The professed goals of this Washington-based health law organization are to ensure that its members are as well informed and effective as possible in their respective professions; to afford members the opportunity to meet with other attorneys and professionals involved in health issues as well as to learn of job vacancies and opportunities in the health care field; to keep members informed of judicial, legislative, and regulatory changes affecting health law; and to provide members in-depth analysis of the most timely issues in health law today.

Initially, NHLA was composed solely of attorneys with an interest or specialty in health care law. In 1983, the organization created an Associate member category to include health professionals. The current membership of approximately 5,000 people includes about 4,000 lawyers, 500 health professionals, and 500 students in law and related graduate fields. With the increase of nonlawyer members, the Association's programs have been modified slightly to make them more reachable to people new to the health law field.

Publications

NHLA has two monthly publications, both of a newsletter format, which are among the best sources in the field for up-to-date information on the legal, regulatory, and political arenas.

Health Law Digest. This digest offers an extensive monthly synopsis of the most current state and federal court decisions on the subject of health law. The information is divided by topic (e.g., antitrust, malpractice, mental health, tax, reimbursement, etc.) and includes many decisions which are either unreported or have not yet appeared in the official advance sheets. Cases and rulings are contributed on a very current basis by member lawyers and others. The *Digest* is structured as a loose-leaf reference service, with monthly updates punched to be inserted into an indexed, segmented binder. An annual case and subject index greatly enhances its effectiveness as a desk reference and legal research tool. A Member's Page distributed with the *Digest* provides information on NHLA activities and members and reports job opportunities in the field of health law. Subscription to the *Digest* is included in the NHLA membership fee; the annual binder is sold for $15.

Health Lawyers News Report. This monthly newsletter tracks and analyzes health-related legislative and regulatory developments at both the state and federal levels.

Programs and Activities

NHLA conducts about a dozen two-day programs each year on focused topics, such as Antitrust in the Health Care Field; Fraud and Abuse; Joint Ventures, Mergers and Acquisitions; Legal and Operational Issues of HMOs, PPOs, and CMPs; Medicare and Medicaid Payment Issues; and Tax Planning. A Health Law Update program held each spring covers a broad range of current topics and provides an excellent overview of what is happening in the health law field. NHLA's conference binders, continue to grow in size and substantive content and are very valuable reference tools, which can be purchased separately from conference registration. Regional luncheons, special mailings of topical literature, a clearinghouse for information on job openings, and career counseling round out NHLA's member services.

Membership Requirements, Types, and Fees

NHLA has three categories of membership; regular, associate, and student. Regular membership is open to any member of the bar who has an interest or practice in the health law field. At $110 per year, the membership includes subscriptions to all NHLA publications, notices of all meetings, and discounts on attendance at educational meetings. Associate membership is open to any health or related professional with an interest in health law or practice. Associate members include physicians and other health professionals, health care administrators, CPAs, financial and benefits managers, association executives, etc. Associate membership is nonvoting but carries all other benefits of regular membership at the same rate. Student membership, at a reduced rate of $20 per year, is open to students in law schools and other graduate programs related to health care.

Contact

David J. Greenburg, Executive Director
National Health Lawyers Association
522 21st Street, NW, Suite 120
Washington, DC 20006
Phone: (202) 833-1100

WORKSHOPS, SYMPOSIA, AND CONFERENCES

Conferences as a mechanism for interaction with peers who share substantive interests and practice experiences are an essential component of an active professionalism. In the preceding section, we have identified some of the conferences sponsored by the major health law organizations. While programs of these national organizations are the easiest to catalogue, they are but a small portion of the overall opportunities for continuing education.

In many regions, groups of health lawyers meet under the auspices of the local bar association to discuss topics of mutual interest. In Boston, for instance, there is a monthly luncheon meeting of health lawyers; in Philadelphia, the bar association's health law committee sponsors a monthly program in the late afternoon. Many other locales offer similar opportunities for professional interaction. In some areas, law schools or health administration programs are the meeting ground for periodic programs on health law topics. There are also several proprietary organizations that put on such programs. For health law teachers in most areas of the country, a small effort at investigation will yield a surprisingly large mix of interesting workshops, symposia, and other meetings involving legal aspects of the health care system. A small, illustrative list of regular programs and sources of program information is provided below.

American Medical Association (AMA)

Twice each year in the *Journal of the American Medical Association (JAMA)*, the AMA prints a listing of courses of interest to medical professionals; a number of these programs involve legal topics. An inquiry addressed to the office of the General Counsel of the AMA would likely yield a similar list.

Aspen Seminars

Aspen Systems Corporation, 1600 Research Blvd., Rockville, MD 20850, is known not only for its extensive list of books, loose-leaf services, and newsletters, but also for its seminars on health law topics, such as health care joint ventures, reimbursement for health care systems, hospital contracts, quality assurance, medical staff law and bylaws, and reorganization of health care systems. The seminars are well organized and conducted, of good quality, and are usually quite detailed on a relatively narrow topic.

The Georgia Hospital Association

The Georgia Hospital Association annually offers two continuing education programs specifically geared toward attorneys: a course on labor relations and an "update" program reviewing the year's additions to the Association's Health Law Manual. Both programs are approved for continuing legal education credit.

The Medical College of Virginia

The Medical College of Virginia's Department of Health Administration and the Veteran's Administration in Richmond, Virginia, jointly sponsor an annual conference on ethical and legal aspects of health care. The College has also, for more than 25 years, held an annual Law Institute on Hospitals and Medicine. This program is designed for a broad health care audience, including executives in health care facilities, physicians, attorneys interested in health law, and students of health administration, law, or medicine. The two-day conference is generally tightly packaged, substantive, and most interesting. The program covers issues such as medical malpractice, product liability, and mergers.

The Practising Law Institute

This national organization for practicing lawyers periodically offers programs on health law topics, often with a forensic focus, such as medical malpractice, liability of health care institutions, and hospital risk management.

The Tennessee Hospital Education and Research Foundation

The Tennessee Hospital Education and Research Foundation presents programs on selected topics throughout the year. Recently, a couse in medical malpractice law was offered on two different dates and in two locations within the state. The program was recommended for administrators, medical staff leaders, staff physicians, hospital trustees, risk management personnel, and nurses. Another program held on multiple occasions by the Foundation covered proper charting of patient care and was directed toward nurses.

HEALTH LAW PUBLICATIONS

Access to sources of legal literature is critical to the health law teacher's ability to stay abreast of the field and provide students with an educational experience that is truly up-to-date. Even faculty members at universities with law libraries may not have access to the broad range of journals and other publications that focus on health law topics. Where the teacher has some input into the library's purchasing and subscription decisions, it is important to know which publications are likely to be the most useful. This section identifies and describes briefly a number of journals and other publications which are of particular value to health law teachers. Although the list is not exhaustive, it covers a good portion of the current health law-related literature. An appendix at the end of this chapter lists other publications worth inspection.

Business and Health. This monthly publication of the Washington Business Group on Health covers a broad range of health care topics and is very useful for obtaining an understanding of industry issues affecting and affected by health law developments. An annual subscription, priced at $79 ($75 prepaid), is available from the Washington Business Group on Health, 229-1/2 Pennsylvania Ave., SE, Washington, DC 20003.

Columbia Journal of Law and Social Problems. Published by the Columbia Law School, Box 73, 435 W. 116th St., New York, NY 10016, this quarterly costs $24 per year. Although not dedicated to health law, the journal deals with legal aspects of social issues and often contains articles related to health law.

Hastings Center Reports. This well-regarded bimonthly journal on bioethics topics frequently contains articles of interest to health law teachers. There is an entire field of bioethics literature that intersects with, and sometimes overlaps substantially, the field of health law. The *Hastings Center Reports*, available at $33 per year (students $28, libraries and institutions $45), are a good representation of this genre. The Hastings Center, 360 Broadway, Hastings-on-Hudson, NY 10706.

Health Affairs. Billed as "a multidisciplinary journal dedicated to the exploration of major domestic and international health policy," this worthwhile new quarterly is edited by John K. Iglehart and published by Project Hope, Millwood, VA 22646. An annual subscription is $24 ($32 for institutions).

Health Care Law: A Practical Guide. This hard-cover loose-leaf service is published by Matther Bender & Co., P.O. Box 658, Albany, NY 12201. The book plus one year of updates is $87.50. This guide covers a broad range of health law issues, including both business and patients' rights aspects. The focus is on the legal practitioner, and practical applications are stressed. Too expensive and detailed for use as a student text, the volume should serve as a useful desk reference for the teacher.

Health Scan. Published 10 times a year by Law and Business, Inc., 855 Valley Road, Clifton, NJ 07013, this newspaper-format journal blends coverage of legal, business and technical issues related to the health care industry. The subscription price is $95 per year.

Hospital Law Manual. This loose-leaf service published by Aspen Systems Corporation, 1600 Research Blvd., Rockville, MD 20850, is a mainstay publication for health law practitioners and health care administrators. Arranged by topics relevant to hospital administration, the service is an excellent reference work for health law teachers with a broader interest than just hospital law. The *Manual* is available in both an administrator's edition and a lawyer's edition; the latter is generally more useful because of the more complete legal citations given for many items. Both editions can be purchased together for $495 annually. The lawyer's edition purchased separately is $420; the administrator's edition is $350. An annual subscription includes periodic updates.

Hospital Law Newsletter. This monthly newsletter, edited by Professor Nathan Hershey of the University of Pittsburgh and published by Aspen Systems, is a useful supplement to the *Hospital Law Manual* and a fine publication in its own right. It summarizes case law and regulatory developments in the field of hospital law and contains valuable articles on such subjects as medical staff relations, institutional liability, and reimbursement issues. An annual subscription is $140. Aspen Systems Corporation, 1600 Research Blvd., Rockville, MD 20850.

Journal of Health Politics, Policy and Law. This well-respected quarterly covers a wide range of health care topics, focusing on the initiation, formulation, and implementation of health policy. Topics covered include politics, sociology, economics, history, psychology, public administration, law, and ethics. The journal is a good source of continuing education materials for teachers and supplemental readings for students. The subscription rate is currently $36 per year (institution $60; student $16). Duke University Press, 6697 College Station, Durham, NC 27708.

Journal of Psychiatry and Law. Dealing with legal issues of psychiatric medicine and mental institutions, this quarterly journal is published by Federal Legal Publications, Inc., 157 Chambers St., New York, NY. The subscription rate is $30 annually.

Medical Trial Technique Quarterly. This quarterly deals with the development of courtroom skills in health-related cases and, more generally, with current laws in this field. The journal is useful to litigation attorneys. Callaghan & Co., 3201 Old Glenview Rd., Wilmette, IL, publishes the journal for $98.50 per year.

New England Journal on Civil and Criminal Confinement. Useful to health lawyers and other professionals working with mental health institutions, this semi-annual journal can be ordered from the New England Journal on Civil and Criminal Confinement, 154 Stuart St., Boston, MA, for $15 per year.

Specialty Law Digest: Health Care. Published monthly by the Bureau of National Affairs, 1231 25th St., NW, Washington, DC, this journal reports court decisions and other developments in health law. A bibliography is included to help readers locate materials on issues of interest to them. A subscription is $272 per year.

State Health Notes. A monthly publication of The George Washington University's Intergovernmental Health Policy Project, *State Health Notes* is edited by Linda Demkovich. This is an excellent publication for keeping track of state legislative and regulatory developments. An annual subscription can be obtained from the Intergovernmental Health Policy Project, 1919 Pennsylvania Ave., NW, Suite 505, Washington, DC 20006.

McGraw Hill's Medicine and Health. Edited by Richard Sorian (formerly by Jerome Brazda, who is now the publisher), this weekly newsletter is the classic "Washington Watch" publication, covering political and legislative developments affecting the health care field. People actively involved in health policy activities consider this "must" reading. A yearly subscription is $327. McGraw Hill Healthcare Information Center, 1120 Vermont Ave., NW, Suite 1200, Washington, DC 20005.

THE HEALTH LAW TEACHER'S ROLE IN CONTINUING EDUCATION

Just as continuing education has much to offer to the health law teacher, the teacher has an important role to play in continuing education for the field of health care administration. Assuming that students receive a sound introduction to the field of health law when going through their basic health administration degree program, there is an obvious need to update this education to keep current with the many changes in the field. Many health administration programs offer various kinds of continuing education activities for their graduates and other practitioners. It is important that these programs contain significant health law content, whether it is organized as a freestanding conference or integrated into programs focused on broader subject areas. The form and content of such programs need not be discussed here; the variety is tremendous, and each health administration program must find the format that best suits its resources and constituencies. Our point here is simply to urge that the need for continuing education in health law topics for program graduates not be overlooked.

APPENDIX

Other Publications Of Interest To Health Law Teachers

Health Care Financial Management contains information on the health care field generally and often has articles dealing with health law topics.

Hospitals (journal of the American Hospital Association), contains a monthly feature titled "Law in Brief."

Journal of the American Dental Association (*JADA*) has a monthly feature entitled "Legislation and Litigation," which covers case law and legislative and regulatory developments.

Journal of the American Medical Association (*JAMA*) contains a monthly feature, "Citation," which covers information of interest to health lawyers.

Modern Healthcare often contains articles on health law-related topics.

New England Journal of Medicine (*NEJM*). Regarded by many as the premier medical professional journal, *NEJM* contains an irregularly recurring feature, "Law-Medicine Notes," written by Professor William J. Curran of the Harvard School of Public Health.

FAH Review (journal of the Federation of American Hospitals, the trade association of the investorowned hospital sector), is a bimonthly and often includes articles on legal topics.

TRADE ASSOCIATION NEWSLETTERS

ACHE News. Published by the American College of Healthcare Executives Communications Department, 840 N. Lake Shore Drive, Chicago, IL on a monthly basis, this newsletter focuses on timely information, varied activities and services of the College, and current news affecting healthcare administrators and lawyers. The subscription price for this newsletter is $5 per year.

The Friday Letter. Published by the Alabama Hospital Association, 500 North East Boulevard, Montgomery, AL, this newsletter is published weekly and focuses on both the state and national legislative changes in the health care field. This information is distributed to the health care manager and lawyer for no additional cost if they are a member of the AlaHA, however, for non-AlaHA members, the cost is $150.

Law Reports (Catholic Health Association, St. Louis, MO). A free newsletter published every six weeks, reporting on laws and issues related to health care.

Perspectives in Hospital and Risk Management. Published by the Society for Hospital Risk Management on a quarterly basis, this newsletter focuses on the recent developments of risk management, medical malpractice, and liability insurance and the implications that these topics will have on the healthcare manager and lawyer. The subscription price of $60 per year includes the membership dues to the Society. The cost per year for students is $35.

LAW FIRM NEWSLETTERS

A rapidly increasing number of law firms engaged in health law practice publish newsletters on health care and health law topics. Most of these are available free of charge upon request to the firm. The following are a small, but representative sampling:

Health Care/Labor Report, Choate, Hall & Stewart (bimonthly), Exchange Place, 53 State Street, Boston, MA 02109.

Mid-Atlantic Health Law Topics, Gordon, Feinblatt, Rothman, Hoffberger & Hollander (quarterly), Garrett Bldg., 233 E. Redwood Street, Baltimore, MD 21202.

Health News Summary, Memel, Jacobs & Ellsworth (monthly), 1801 Century Park East, 25th Floor, Los Angeles, CA 90067.

Health Law Update, Wolf, Block, Schorr & Solis-Cohen (quarterly), Packard Bldg., Philadelphia, PA 19102.

CHAPTER 9

HEALTH LAW COURSE OUTLINES

FALL QUARTER, 1985
HEALTH LAW: HA 513

Faculty: Darryl Eugene Crompton, J.D., M.P.H.
Associate Professor, DHSA, Ext. 5661
University of Alabama, Birmingham

Class Schedule: Monday 10:00 am - 12:00 pm
Wednesday 8:00 am - 10:00 am

1. *Course Objectives*:

    A. To familiarize students with the nature, perspectives and objectives of the legal process.

    B. To provide skills in understanding legal terminology, legal reasoning, and to understand the legal constraints upon management decision making within the health care sector.

    C. To increase a manager's ability to recognize legal issues, to read a legal case, to approach and research statutes, regulations and case law, and to be intelligent consumers of legal services in health organizations.

2. *Readings*:

    Southwick, Arthur, *The Legal Aspects of Health Care Administration*.
    Cook, Robin, *Mindbend*.
    In-class reading materials.

3. *Course Requirements*:

    Legal Bibliography Working Papers   50%

Midterm Examination	20%
Final Examination	20%
Class Participation	10%

4. *Legal Bibliography*:

One of the main strengths of HA 513 is the exposure of graduate students to both primary and secondary legal literature. Ten legal bibliographical working papers, each worth 5% of your final course grade, have been designed to help you explore the legal literature and at the same time integrate that literature into a health administrative context. All working papers will be typewritten, comply with either GPHHA or APA writing guidelines and be turned in by the assigned deadline.

Bib Titles	*Due Dates*
Bib 1 - *Mindbend* Think Paper	September 23
Bib 2 - *Canterbury* Think Paper	September 25
Bib 3 - Legal Terminology	September 30
Bib 4 - Alabama Code	October 7
Bib 5 - Reporters	October 14
Bib 6 - Digests	October 21
Bib 7 - Regulations	October 28
Bib 8 - Law Review Article	November 4
Bib 9 - AL	November 11
Bib 10 - Praxis	November 18

5. *Course Units:*   *Readings*:

W	Overview of Course	*Mindbend*
M*	Introduction to Law	*Canterbury*, S:1-28
W*	Ethics	*Canterbury*, S:1-28
M*	Statutory Law	In-class
W	Case Law	In-class
M*	Civil and Criminal Law/Litigation	In-class
W	Corporate Law	S:29-59
M*	Corporate Law	In-class

W	Contracts Law	S:89-111
M*	Tort Law	S:112-158
W	Tort Law	In-class
M*	Tort Law	In-class
W	Agency Law	In-class
M*	MIDTERM EXAMINATION	
W	Medical Record Law	S:298-345
M*	Medical Record Law	In-class
W	Patients Rights Law	S:159-259
M*	Praxis Presentations/ Course Review	
Th	FINAL EXAMINATION	S:159-259

* Denotes dates working papers due

HSA 542 - Health Care Jurisprudence

Fall Semester 1985   Professor M.J. Dundas
TTh 4:45 - 6:00   Arizona State University

Course Description

The students will examine the legal problems relating to health care facilities. The course provides a basic framework for analysis of contemporary legal issues in health law.

Objectives

The course is designed to examine a number of legal problems so that the students will:

1. Become acquainted with the basic legal principles and their application to health care services;

2. Be able to recognize the legal responsibilities inherent in the role of the health care administrator;

3. Become familiar with legal literature.

Course Requirements

1. A scholarly paper on a specific health care issue with emphasis on the legal ramifications of the health care institution. The paper will include the historical development; the current status of the legal problem; alternatives available to the health care facility; recommendations; a review of legal cases and statutes where applicable; and bibliography. The students will use *Uniform System of Citations*, 13th ed., when citing legal materials.

2. Presentation of the selected problem to the class. The student is expected to discuss as well as answer problems arising in the following discussion period.

3. Mid-term and final examinations consisting of essay questions.

4. *Evaluation*

Paper, presentation, and discussion	33%
Mid-term	33%
Final examination	33%

5. Method of student presentation. Each student will select a current contemporary issue to present to the class. A tentative topic with outline will be submitted on September 10. The final selection of the problem and the presentation date will be made by September 17. The presentation will be made on Tuesday. On Thursday, the issues raised on Tuesday will be discussed. Each student will select applicable portions of the texts to be read *and* a minimum of two articles on the topic for the class to read.

These articles will be made available *two weeks* ahead of the presentation date. One copy will be left in the HSA Department and one article will be left in the ADS Department. Each member of the class will be expected to read the articles prior to the class. The articles may be read at the Department Office, or the student may check out the articles for a 1/2 hour period to copy the articles. Each student will submit their articles in a marked folder, with an attached sign-out sheet in the following format:

Name   Time Out   Time Returned

The folder will be marked with the name of the article, the student's name, and telephone number.

Three presentations will be given on each Tuesday, therefore, students should try to present issues that are compatible on the same Tuesday. The dates of presentations are October 15, 22, 29, and November 5, 12, 19 and December 3. Each student will have approximately 25 minutes to make the presentation. However, the three students may agree among themselves to divide the time in any manner, but no student may take less than 15 minutes. A presentation panel is acceptable. On Thursday, the three students who presented the issues the previous Tuesday will lead a discussion panel on the issues presented.

Course Text

Miller, Robert D. *Problems in Hospital Law*, Fourth Edition, Aspen Systems Corporation, 1983.

Whitman & Gergacz. *The Legal and Social Environment of Business*, Random House, 1985.

Course Outline

Introduction to Law   Preface, Chap 1

	Chap 1
Introduction to Courts	Chap 2
	Chap 1
Law Library Tour	Law Library
Litigation	Chaps 3, 4, 5
Contracts	Chap 7
	Chap 10
Commercial Paper	Handout
Secured Transactions	Handout
Torts	Chap 8
Medical Malpractice Statutes and Cases	Chaps 10, 11
Continued	
Midterm	
Corporations and Corporate Governance	Chap 12
	pp 343-349
	Chap 2
Regulation and Accreditation	Chap 3
Agency	Handout
Medical Staff	Chap 7
Staff Relations	Chap 9
Patient Relations	Chap 12
Informed Consent	Chap 13
Continued	
Medical Records	Chap 14
Confidentiality	Chap 14
Dying and Death	Chap 16
Withholding or Termination for Treatment	Chap 16
Human Experimentation	
Reproductive Issues	Chap 15
Thanksgiving	
Reorganization and Closure	Chap 6
Antitrust	Chaps 13, 14, 15
Future Trends	Chap 16
	Chap 5
Papers due	
Continued	
Final examination	

Legal Aspects of Health Care - BA 954

Fall Term 1985
TTh 1:30 - 3:00
Arnold J. Rosoff, J.D.
The University of Pennsylvania, The Wharton School

GENERAL DESCRIPTION:

The laws affecting health care delivery in the United States are in a process of substantial and inconsistent change. In many respects, the health care industry is continuing its transformation from an unregulated non-system to a tightly regulated service industry, not unlike a public utility. In other ways, a strong movement toward open competition and free enterprise is being encouraged. Both of these trends involve changes in the law and regulatory initiatives which are important, complex, and highly interesting. The study of how courts, legislatures, and administrative agencies, at both the state and federal levels, are attempting to guide--or at least keep pace with--changes in the health care system gives fascinating insight into the law's ability to serve and affect complex social systems. Of more specific concern to the health care manager are the many ways in which the law constrains managerial decision-making. There is scarcely an area of managerial activity in health care upon which the law does not have significant impact.

BA 954 attempts both a historical and current overview of legal regulation of the health care enterprise. By following developments from the past to the present, it is possible to gain insight into what will likely come about in the future. Of particular interest are the social, ethical, and public policy issues the law addresses in trying to balance the rights of individuals against the needs and concerns of a modern society.

COURSE FORMAT:

The course combines lecture by the instructor with substantial group discussion. The setting is informal and the class is encouraged to participate actively.

COURSE REQUIREMENTS AND GRADING:

The course entails a mid-term exam (30%), a substantial legal research project and paper (30%), and a final exam (30%). Class participation is also considered in grading (10%).

PREREQUISITES:

There is no formal prerequisite for the course, although most Health Care Administration majors take the course in their second year and thus have had several of the basic HCA courses. A background knowledge of the health care system is extremely helpful for full appreciation of the issues covered in BA 954. Interested students not in the Health Care major should consult the instructor before enrolling in the course.

COURSE MATERIALS:

The text is Curran & Shapiro, *Law, Medicine and Forensic Science*, Third Edition (Little, Brown & Co., Boston, 1982). Supplementary materials will be sold through the Wharton Duplicating Center.

Class 1   September 5 - Introduction
1. Course objectives, methodology, materials and grading
2. Insights into the Law-Medicine Interface
3. Overview: the American legal system

Class 2A   September 10 - Medical Malpractice: Basic Principles
1. Professional standards and liability
2. Contract vs. tort theories
3. Errors of judgment

4. Good samaritan laws
5. Statutes of limitation

Text: pp. 345-347 (bkgd), 351-364, 390-395, 481-502

Class 2B September 12 - Institutional Responsibility
1. Hospitals and other health care facilities
2. Vicarious liability and corporate responsibility
3. Res ipsa loguitur and negligence per se
4. Immunity defenses, releases of liability

Class 3A September 17 - The Malpractice Crisis and Reforms
1. The liability insurance industry
2. The nature and extent of the "crisis"
3. Statutory reforms and constitutional issues
4. The risk management movement
5. Alternative dispute resolution (ADR) innovations

Text: pp. 517-549, 561-569, 573-577, 585-592
Supp: materials to be assigned

Class 3B September 19 - Special Class: Tour of Law Library

Class 4A September 24 - Informed Consent: Principles
1. Old and new standards for disclosure to patients
2. What price self-determination?
3. Latitude for professional discretion

Text: pp. 411-435, 463-465, 474-480

Class 4B September 26 - Informed Consent: Practice
1. The role of intermediaries
2. Problems of documentation
3. Patients' perceptions
4. Statutory reforms

Text: pp. 457-463, 466-473, 569-573

Class 5A October 1 - Open

Class 5B October 3 - Governmental Regulation of Professional Practice
1. Education, testing and licensure
2. Discipline of problem professionals
3. Non-MD health professionals
4. Regulating professional-patient interactions

Text: pp. 593-618
Supplementary cases: *Barber v. Reinking, Landeros v. Flood, Tarasoff v. Regents*

Class 6A October 8 - Regulation by the Health Professions
1. Professional societies and certification
2. Hospital staff privileges and peer review
3. Professional regulation and competition

Text: pp. 618-644

Class 6B October 10 - Labor Relations in the Health Sector
1. Overview: labor-management relations
2. The NLRA, NLRB, and the 1974 Labor Amendments
3. Health care unionization and collective bargaining
4. Strikes and grievance mechanisms

Materials: to be assigned

Class 7A October 15 - Open

Class 7B October 17 - Mid-Term Exam, In Class, All Material to Date

Class 8A October 22 - No Class; Fall Break

Class 8B October 24 - Access to Health Services
1. A duty to treat?
2. The public-private distinction
3. State statutory requirements
4. Federal funding, tax, and access policy

Text: pp. 644-661, 904-917

Text: pp. 644-661, 904-917
Supp: *Wilmington Gen'l Hosp. v. Manlove, Cook v. Ochsner*

Note: By this date, all students must turn in one-page proposals on term research topics for instructor review

Class 9A October 29 - Health Planning and Certification of Need
1. Controlling cost through capital investment
2. The Certificate of Need movement
3. Federal initiatives, P.L. 93-641 and beyond

Text: pp. 661-677, 694-698
Supp: *North Carolina v. Califano*

Class 9B October 31 - Cost Containment Initiatives
1. Medicare and Medicaid: "going-in assumptions"
2. The search for control levers
3. Rate-setting and prospective payment strategies
4. A quality/cost trade-off?

Text: pp. 708-747
Supp: Eisenberg & Rosoff, "Physician Responsibility for the Cost of Unnecessary Medical Services"

Class 10A November 5 - Competition: New Opportunities and Issues
1. The medical-industrial complex
2. The "corporate practice of medicine"
3. Medicare/Medicaid fraud and abuse provisions
4. Other state and federal restrictions

Materials to be assigned

Class 10B November 7 - Antitrust Issues in the Health Industry
1. Federal jurisdiction through the "commerce power"
2. Price fixing
3. Monopolies and exclusive arrangements
4. Health planning as "restraint of trade"

Text: pp. 677-685, 692-707 (review 694-698, prev. assigned)
Supp: *Arizona v. Maricopa County Med. Soc'y*, *Hyde v. Jefferson Parish*, other materials to be assigned

Class 11A November 12 - Control Through the Insurance Mechanism
1. Insurance regulation: McCarren Act and the state role
2. Insurance departments: authority and practical limits
3. Treatment of the "Blues" and new forms of health plans
4. ERISA preemption issues

Materials to be assigned

Class 11B November 14 - Open

Class 12A November 19 - Tax Law
1. Tax exemption for health care organizations
2. Obtaining tax-exempt status: the mechanics
3. "Unrelated business income"
4. Relations between non-profit and for-profit entities

Text: pp. 651-657 (prev. assigned)
Supp: materials to be assigned

Class 12B November 21 - Open: Return and Discuss Mid-Term Exams

Class 13A November 26 - Refusal of Treatment
1. Self-determination: the right to decide for one's self
2. Treating minors and incompetents
3. Problems with "substituted judgment"
4. Terminal and hopeless patients

Text: pp. 777-839 (recommended 853-877)
Supp: *In re Conroy*

Class 13B   November 28 - No Class; Thanksgiving

Class 14A   December 3 - Sexual and Procreative Issues
1. Sexual behavior and the "right of privacy"
2. Abortion and fetal rights
3. Parental, spousal, and societal rights
4. Government funding of sex-related care

Text: pp. 879-917 (904-917 prev. assigned)
Supp: *Roe v. Wade*

Note: Term Research Papers Must Be Turned In By This Date

Class 14B   December 5 - Organ Transplantation and Donation
1. High-tech miracles raise new issues
2. Organ donation: the UAGA, donations by incompetents
3. Obtaining an adequate supply of transplantable organs
4. Economic realities and societal choices

Text: pp. 1010-1054

Final Exam: Date, Time and Location to be announced
Coverage: All Materials Since Mid-Term Exam

Legal Studies 11 / Health Care 11
Health Care and the Rights of Citizens

Spring 1986
TTh 9:00 - 10:20
Arnold J. Rosoff, J.D.
The University of Pennsylvania, The Wharton School

Text: Curran and Shapiro, *Law, Medicine and Forensic Science*, 3rd ed. (Little, Brown, 1982). Duplicated supplementary readings will be assigned during the course.

Grading: Mid-term (30%); Final (30%); Research Project (30%); Class participation (10%); extra-credit writing options.

Writing Assistance: The course participates in the Writing Across the University (WATU) program and offers expert assistance to students in improving their communications skills. Students' participation in WATU activities is optional and voluntary.

Jan. 14   Course introduction: overview -- health care, the law, and individual rights

Jan. 16   Principles of malpractice law
pp. 351-69 (pp. 345-51 suggested as background)

Jan. 21   Malpractice (cont.), pp. 369-411

Jan. 23   Informed consent: concept and principles; pp. 411-35

Jan. 28   Informed consent to research and experimental care; pp. 436-56

Jan. 30   Informed consent: practical considerations; pp. 457-73

Feb. 4   The "malpractice crisis" and proposed solutions; pp. 517-22, 535-49, 573-77, 583-92

Feb. 6   Open – a special session will be held at an agreed time to view "The Verdict" (with Paul Newman). A short, ungraded writing assignment on issues raised in the movie will be reviewed by the instructor and a WATU writing consultant.

Feb. 11   Special Class – tour of Biddle Law Library

Feb. 13   Abortion: the right established; *Roe v. Wade* and other materials to be assigned

Feb. 18   Abortion: further issues, pp. 886-917

Feb. 20   Family planning, contraception, and minors' rights; pp. 879-86 and supplementary materials to be assigned

NOTE: By this date, students must submit a short proposal to allow instructor review/approval of their research projects.

Feb. 25   Open

Feb. 27   Mid-term exam, in class; all material to date

Mar. 4   Protecting the public's health: the police power; materials to be assigned

Mar. 6   Public health: the dilemma of AIDS; pp. 611-13, 615-18 and other materials to be assigned

Mar. 11 and Mar. 13 – Spring Break

Mar. 18   Access to care: the practitioner's duty to treat; pp. 608-11, 488-94

Mar. 20   Access: the institution's duty to treat; pp. 644-61

NOTE: Drafts/outlines due from students participating in WATU

Mar. 25   Open

Mar. 27   Balancing cost, access and quality: inevitable trade-offs? pp. 661-77 and supplementary materials

Apr. 1   Competition in health care: changes and new issues; materials to be assigned

Apr. 3   High-tech care: organ transplants; pp. 1014-34 (skim pp. 1036-48) plus supplementary materials

Apr. 8   Open

Apr. 10   Refusal of treatment: recognizing the right; pp. 803-22

Apr. 15   Deciding for incompetents and the terminally ill; pp. 822-77

Apr. 17   Deciding on treatment for newborns; materials to be assigned

Apr. 22   Open

Apr. 24   Open; wrap-up and review for final exam

Final Exam - Date, Time, and Place to be announced

H.A. 652 - Legal Aspects of Hospital and Health Care Administration

Arthur F. Southwick, J.D.
The University of Michigan
Program in Hospital Administration
School of Public Health

Required Text:

    Southwick (with George J. Siedel), *Law of Hospital and Health Care Administration*, Health Administration Press, University of Michigan, 1978. (On reserve in both Public Health and Bus. Ad. Library.) (Available for purchase from the Press.)

Readings (both required and optional):

    Quimby, *Law for the Medical Practitioner*, Health Administration Press, Ann Arbor, 1979.

    Hospital Law Manual, Administrator's Volume, Health Law Center, Aspen Systems Corporation.

    Miller, *Problems in Hospital Law*, Fourth Edition, Aspen Systems Corporation, 1983.

    Black's Law Dictionary.

    Gifis, *Law Dictionary*, Barron's Educational Series.

    Pozgar, *Legal Aspects of Health Care Administration*, Second Edition, Aspen Systems Corporation, 1983.

    Annas, et al., *Rights of Doctors, Nurses, and Allied Health Professionals*, Avon, 1981.

    Christoffel, *Health and the Law, Macmillan, 1982.*

    Action Kit for Hospital Law, John F. Horty, Esq., Editor. (This is a loose leaf book revised and supplemented periodically plus a monthly report analyzing recent court decisions.)

Peters, Fineberg, Kroll, *Law of Medical Practice in Michigan*, Health Administration Press, Ann Arbor, 1981.

Hayt, *Medicolegal Aspects of Hospital Records*, Physicians Record Co. 2d edition, 1977.

Peters, Fineberg, Kroll, Collins, *Anesthesiology and the Law*, Health Administration Press, Ann Arbor, 1983.

Fineberg, Peters, Wilson, Kroll, *Obstetrics/Gynecology and the Law*, Health Administration Press, Ann Arbor, 1984.

Shaw and Doudera, *Defining Human Life*, AUPHA Press, Ann Arbor, 1984.

Doudera and Swazey, *Refusing Treatment in Mental Health Institutions - Values in Conflict*, AUPHA Press, 1982.

Doudera and Peters, *Legal and Ethical Aspects of Treating Critically and Terminally Ill Patients*, AUPHA Press, Ann Arbor, 1982.

Lidz, Meissel, et al., *Informed Consent: A Study of Decision Making in Psychiatry*, Guilford Press, New York, 1984.

Part I - Introduction to Law and Legal Process

Sept. 9   Law Defined and Classified, Constitutional Law, Legislation; preface pg. v-viii, pp. 3-12.

Sept. 11   Sources of Law--Common Law and Equity, Contract and Torts; pp. 3-12

Sept. 16   Federal and State Court Systems; pp. 13-28

Part II - The Physician-Patient Relationship

Sept. 18   Creation of Relationship, Breach of Contract, Intentional Tort; pp. 91-111

Sept. 23   Negligence--Standards of Care and Breach of Duty, Proximate Cause; pp. 112-143

Sept. 25   Negligence (cont.), Damages for Mental Anguish; pp. 112-143, 371-378

Sept. 30   Statutory Reforms of Tort System, Arbitration; pp. 143-158

Part III - The Health Care Institution as a Corporation

Oct. 2   Nature of a Corporation, Corporate Authority, Corporate Practice of Medicine--HMO's; pp. 31-40

Oct. 7   Corporate Mgmt--Officers and Agents, Fiduciary Duties of Members of Board; pp. 40-57

Oct. 9   Charitable Status, Federal Taxation; pp. 58-79

Oct. 14   State Taxation of Real Estate; pp. 79-87

Oct. 16   Corporate Reorganization and Multi-Hospital Systems

Part IV - The Hospital-Patient Relationship

Oct 21   Mid-Term Exam

Oct. 23   Consent for Treatment; pp. 203-228

Oct. 28   Refusal of Consent: Competent and Incompetent Patients, "Right-to-Die" Legislation; pp. 228-237

Oct. 30	Consent--Minors, Refusal of Parents to Consent; pp. 237-250
Nov. 4	Abortion; pp. 260-284
Nov. 6	Sterilization, Cause for Action for "Wrongful Life" and "Wrongful Birth"; pp. 285-297
Nov. 11	Medical Records - Confidentiality; pp. 298-335
Nov. 13	Medical Records - Use as Evidence, Freedom of Information Acts, Discoverability by Third Parties; pp. 335-345
Nov. 18	Hospital Liability - Emergency Care - Respondent Superior; pp. 182-202, 346-399
Nov. 20	Borrowed Servant, Nursing Negligence
Nov. 25	Hospital Liability--Corporate Negligence and Negligence in Selection of Medical Staff; pp. 399-423
Nov. 27	Licensing--Nurse Practitioners and Physician Assistants Scope of Practice

Part V - The Hospital-Physician Relationship

Dec. 2	Medical Staff Appointments Public and Private Hospitals; pp. 427-465
Dec. 4	Delineation and Control of Medical Staff Privileges, Due Process of Law, Medical Staff By-laws
Dec. 9	Medical Staff Privileges, Antitrust Litigation
Dec. 11	Quality Assurance Programs, Medical Staff Committee Records, Confidentiality and Immunity
Dec. 20	Final Examination

Grade determined by:

    Examination, Oct. 21 = 100 points
    Examination, Dec. 20 = 100 points
    Term Paper   = 100 points
    Class Participation = 50 points

    Total   = 350 points

In determining grade for class participation, the instructor shall use discretion based upon the student's analysis of the assigned cases, ability to suggest solutions to hypothetical cases, and expression of understanding the conflicting social, political, and economic considerations that determine the ultimate outcome of litigation. Points will be recorded by intervals of 5. To measure fairly an individual's participation, the instructor shall make notations from time to time throughout the semester.

Excessive absences from class (more than 3 or 4) will necessarily preclude a "good" grade for class participation. Please see me if illness or family emergency cause more than a random absence from class.

Make-up examinations will be given only if illness, family emergency, or extraordinary good cause prevents your attendance. Please mark your calendars now reserving the examination dates and plan your travel schedule accordingly.

Master List of Cases and Articles

Part I - Introduction to Law and Legal Process

1. *Brown v. Board of Education of Topeka*, 347 U.S. 686, 74 S. Ct. 686 (1954).
2. *Yick Wo v. Hopkins*, 118 U.S. 356, 6 S. Ct. 1064 (1886).
3. *Jackson v. Edison Co.*, 419 U.S. 345, 95 S. Ct. 449 (1974).
4. *Woods v. Lancet*, 303 N.Y. 349, 102 N. E. 2d 691 (1951).

5. *Burch v. State of Louisiana*, 99 S. Ct. 1623 (1979).

Part II - The Physician-Patient Relationship

6. *Oliver v. Brock*, 342 So. 2d 1 (Alabama 1976).
7. *Stevens v. Kimmel*, 349 N. E. 2d 232 (Ind. Ct. App. 1979).
8. *Guy v. Thomas*, 55 Ohio St. 2d 183, 378 N. E. 2d 488 (1978).
9. *Perin v. Hayne*, 210 N. W. 2d 609 (Iowa 1973).
10. *Helling v. Carey*, 519 P. 2d 981, 83 Wash. 2d 514 (1974).
11. *Beatty v. Akron City Hospital*, 67 Ohio St. 2d 483 (1981).

Part III - The Health Care Institution as a Corporation

12. *Charlotte Hungerford Hospital v. Mulvey*, 26 Conn. Sup. 394, 225 A. 2d 495 (1966).

13. *Komanetsky v. Missouri State Medical Assoc.*, 516 S. W. 2d 545 (Mo. 1975).

14. *Stern v. Lucy Webb Hayes National Training School*, 381 F. Supp. 1003 (D.C.D.C. 1974).

15. *HCSC - Laundry v. U.S.*, 101 S. Ct. 836 (1981).

16. *Greater Anchorage Area Borough v. Sisters of Charity*, 553 P. 2d 467 (1976).

17. *Ex Parte Baker*, 432 So. 2d 1281 (Ala. 1983).

18. *Woodyard v. Arkansas Diversified Ins. Co.*, 594 S. W. 2d 13 (1980).

   Article: Roach, "Hospitals Reorganize to Survive the 80's", *Hospitals*, March 1, 1982, pg. 78 et seq.

   Article: Kopit, "Hospitals Must Consider Antitrust Implications of Multi-Institutional Arrangements", *Hospitals*, March 1, 1982, pg. 82 et seq.

Part IV - The Hospital - Patient Relationship

19. *Rogers v. Lumbermens Mutual Casualty Co.*, 119 So. 2d 649 (1960).

20. *DiFilippo v. Preston*, 173 A. 2d 333 (1961).

21. *Harcish v. Children's Hospital*, 439 N. E. 2d 240 (Mass. 1982).

    Article: Brant, "Last Rights: An Analysis of Refusal and Withholding of Treatment of Cases," *Missouri Law Review*, Vol. 46, pg. 338, (1981).

22. *Kirby v. Spivey*, 307 S. E. 2d 538 (Ga. CA 1983).

23. *Leach v. Akroon City Hospital*, 68 Ohio Misc. 1 (1980).

24. *Barber v. Superior Court*, 195 Cal. Rptr. 484 (Ct. App. 1983).

    Article: Finamore, "Jefferson v. Griffin Spalding Hospital Authority: Court Ordered Surgery to Protect Life of an Unborn Child", *American Journal of Law and Medicine*, Vol. 9, No. 1, pg. 83-101.

Abortion and Sterilization

    Article: Warren, "The Law of Human Reproduction", *Journal of Legal Medicine*, Vol. 3, No. 1, pg. 1, March 1982.

25. *City of Akron v. Akron Center for Reproductive Health, Inc.*, 103 S. Ct. 2481 (1983).

    Article: Baron, "Fetuses and the Concept of Person

in the Law", *Law, Medicine and Health Care*, April 1983, pg. 52-63; 81.

26. *Harbeson v. Parke-Davis*, 98 Wash. 2d 460, 656 P.2d 483 (1983).

Medical Records

27. *Horne v. Paton*, 291 Ala. 701, 287 So. 2d 824 (1973).

28. *Estate of Berthiaume v. Pratt, M.D.*, 365 A. 2d 792 (Maine 1976).

Hospital Liability

Emergency Care

29. *Fjerstad v. Knutson*, 271 N. W. 2d 8 (S. D. 1978).

30. *Cooper C. Curry*, 92 N.M. 417, 589 P. 2d 201 (1978).

31. *Hannola v. City of Lakewood*, 68 Ohio App. 2d 61 (1980).

32. *Tonsic v. Wagner*, 329 A. 2d 497 (1974).

33. *Norton v. Argonaut Insurance Co.*, 144 So. 2d 249 (La. C.A. 1962).

34. *Johnson v. Misericordia Community Hospital*, 301 N.W. 2d 156 (Wisconsin 1981).

35. *Elam v. College Park Hospital*, Court of Appeal, California, 1982.

   Article: Southwick, "Hospital Liability: Two Theories Have Been Merged", *Journal of Legal Medicine*, Vol. 4, No. 1, March 1983, pp. 1-50.

Licensing

   Article: Wolff, "Court Upholds Expanded Practice

Roles for Nurses", *Law, Medicine, and Health Care*, Feb. 1984, pg. 26-29.

Part V - The Hospital-Physician Relationship

36. *Griesman v. Newcomb Hospital*, 40 N.J. 389, 192 A. 2d 817 (1963).

37. *Moore v. Board of Trustees of Carson-Tahoe Hospital*, 495 P. 2d 605 (Nevada 1972).

38. *Garrow v. Elizabeth General Hospital*, 79 N.J. 549, 401 A. 2d 533 (1979).

   Article: Southwick, "The Physician's Right to Due Process in Public and Private Hospitals: Is There a Difference?" *Medicolegal News*, Vol. 9, No. 1, February 1981, pp. 4-9; 29.

   Draft
   Article: Southwick, "Anti-Trust Litigation in the American Health Care Industry", pages 39-64.

   Article: Southwick and Slee, "Quality Assurance in Health Care: Confidentiality and Immunity for Participants", *Journal of Legal Medicine*, Fall 1984.

   Article: Nord, "Antitrust Law and Exclusive Contracts: Obstacles to Patients' Benefits?" *Law, Medicine, and Health Care*, April 1983, pp. 64-70.

HA 348 LAW FOR HEALTH ADMINISTRATION

Professor David Warren
Department of Health Administration
Duke University Medical Center

Objectives:

To acquaint health administration students with current and future legal and policy issues in the health care field, through an examination of laws, regulations, court decisions and the legal process.

To develop skills in understanding legal terminology, identifying legal issues and determining when to obtain legal assistance.

To demonstrate the relevance of law in solving management problems and making health policy decisions, both in theory and in practice.

Methods:

Lectures and class discussion.

Memorandum (10-15 pp.) researched and written on the application of law to a specific health policy issue or institutional management problem; presentation of memo topic as a 10 minute legal briefing in class.

Quizzes - weekly, based on assigned readings.

Final Exam - objective and subjective questions based on the principal texts and lectures.

Grade - 40% memorandum; 40% final exam; 10% quizzes; 10% memo presentation.

Materials:

American Society of Hospital Attorneys, *Federal Regulation: Hospital Attorneys' Desk Reference* (1980)

Annas, Glantz, Katz, *The Rights of Doctors, Nurses and Allied Health Professions* (1981)

Christofel, *Health and the Law* (1982)

Havighurst, "Contributions of Antitrust Law to a Procompetitive Health Policy" in *Market Reforms in Health Care* (1983) (Handout)

Kaluzny, Warner, Warren & Zelman, *Management of Health Services* (1982) (On Reserve)

*Miller, *Problems in Hospital Law*, 4th Ed. (1983) ("Problems") (Bookstore)

President's Commission for the Study of Ethical Problems in Medicine and Biomedical and Behavioral Research, *Defining Death* (1981) (On Reserve)

Southwick, *The Law of Hospital and Health Care Administration* (1978)

Warren, "Medical Malpractice in the USA" in *Medical Malpractice* (1980) ("Malpractice Paper") (Handout)

Warren, "Patient Medical Information and Records in the U.S.: Disclosure and Access" in *Health Law in Canada* (1981) (Handout)

Warren, "The Law of Human Reproduction: An Overview" in *The Journal of Legal Medicine* (1982) ("Overview") (Handout)

*Wing, *The Law and the Public's Health*, 2d edition (1985) ("Wing") (Bookstore)

*Required books - Bookstore

Course Outline

Why law is important in health administration, Case (Handout), Book reviews (Handout)

Introduction to Liability Issues, Problems 1, 10, 11, Wing, 1

Responding to Liability (Diosegy), Malpractice Paper, Wing, 1

Governance/Administration, Problems, 2, Wing, 10

Accreditation/Licensure, Problems, 3, 8

Regulation, Problems, 5, Wing, 2, 6, 7

Antitrust, Problems, pp. 58-61, Wing, 8, Havighurst paper

Authorization for Treatment, Problems, 13

Confidentiality/Disclosure/Patient Information, Patient Medical Information (Diosegy), Handout, Problems, 14

Alternative Delivery Systems (Hastings), Problems, 6

Corporate Reorganization, Handout

Contractual Relationships with Patients, Problems, 12

Financial Accountability/Taxation & Exemption, Problems, 4

NO CLASS

Medical Staff-Standards (Diosegy), Problems pp. 84-95, Problems, 7

Medical Staff - Organization/Liability, Handout

Legal Memo Due

Medical Staff/Management Relations, Cases (Handout)

Legal Ethical Issues/Reproduction, Problems, 15, Wing, 4

Legal Ethical Issues - Dying, Problems, 16, Presidential Commission Report

Unions and Collective Bargaining, Problems pp. 165-176

Employee Relations (Ratliff), Problems pp. 157-165

Memo Presentations

Memo Presentations

Memo Presentations

Memo Presentations

Future Legal Issues in Health Administration, Wing, 5 (Wing)

Final Examination

Guest Lecturers

Arlene J. Diosegy, Assistant University Counsel, Duke University Medical Center; Douglas A. Hastings, Attorney with Epstein, Becker, Borsody & Green, Washington, D.C.; Kenneth Wing, Associate Professor, School of Law and School of Public Health, University of North Carolina-Chapel Hill; Ernest Ratliff, Attorney in Raleigh and Clinton (former faculty member at UNC-CH and NC Central).

APPENDIX

*Bibliography from the
Journal of Health Politics, Policy and Law*

Research Note

CURRENT RESOURCES FOR HEALTH LAW RESEARCH

Abstract. This article reports on a conference held at Duke University in October 1985. It presents an introductory discussion of the growth and complexity of health law literature and includes an extensive bibliography of health law information sources and descriptive summaries of health law databases.

INTRODUCTION
David G. Warren, Duke University

Recognizing that health law is a rapidly growing field, both commercially and academically,[1] Duke University hosted a symposium (October 21-22, 1985, in Durham, N.C.) entitled "New Developments in Database Resources for Health Law." Invited were law and medical librarians and health law teachers from medical schools, law schools, and health administration programs at universities in the mid-Atlantic region. The goal of participants was to discuss and critique existing bibliographies and research aids for the health law field[2] and examine new technologies that are becoming available to health law researchers. An unusual feature of the symposium was the on-site comparison of two new computer-based bibliographic search systems--one from the University of Alberta, the other from the American Hospital Association. Because of this cross-cultural emphasis, funding for the meeting was provided by the Canadian Studies Center at Duke University through a grant from the U.S. Department of Education.

Symposium participants were presented with a review of relevant medical library resources, including the electronic databases MEDLINE (based largely on *Index Medicus*) and HEALTH (a counterpart to the *Hospital Literature Index*), by Elizabeth Adams, Reference Librarian at the Duke Medical Center Library. The development of the University of Alberta's health law electronic research system was explained and demonstrated by one of its developers, Martin P.J. Kratz, who is now a barrister and solicitor in Edmonton, Alberta. HEALTHLAWYER, the new online health care bibliographic database produced by the American Hospital Association, was described by Richard L. Epstein, AHA Senior Vice President, and demonstrated by Azike A. Ntephe, Director of the AHA Office of Legal Communications. Other computer-based legal research services were also demonstrated, including LEXIS, NEXIS, and MEDIS (Mead Data Central), WESTLAW (West Publishing Company) and LegalTrac Database (Information Access Corporation). These systems are not designed specifically for health law materials, but they can be used to access health law topics. The current status of health law research resources was presented by Richard Danner, Director of the Library, and Claire Germain, Assistant Librarian of Duke University's School of Law.

It is apparent that numerous tools now exist for performing research on topics associated with the health law field. The competition among both commercial vendors and nonprofit suppliers has been a boon to researchers in this growing field. Comparisons among the many sources of information reveal both duplication and complementary uses. The following sections describe the diverse sources available to the health law researcher.

Notes

1. C.D. Stromberg, "Health Law Comes of Age: Economics and Ethics in a Changing Industry," *Yale Law Journal* 92 (November 1982):203-17; D.G. Warren, Review Essay, "The Coming of Age of Health Law: A Review of Recent Textbooks," *Journal of Health Politics, Policy and Law* 8 (Summer 1983):387-95; and C.J. Schramm and M.S. Hencke, Research Note, "The Teaching of Health Law in 1980: Results of a Survey," *Journal of Health Politics, Policy and Law* 6 (Fall 1981):558-59.
2. See W.J. Curran, "Titles in the Medicolegal Field: A Proposal for Reform," *American Journal of Law and*

Medicine 1 (March 1975):1-11. This historical analysis of terminology used in Britain and America presents a set of defined terms for use "with respect to interdisciplinary discourse in the broad field of medico-legal relations." While suggesting "legal medicine" for the medical side and "medical law" for the legal side, and calling "medical jurisprudence" inappropriate for any purpose, Professor Curran proposes the broader title "health law" to cover the broad-ranging legal aspects of medicine, nursing, dentistry, and other health service fields, including public health and the environment.

MEDICAL LIBRARY INFORMATION SERVICES FOR HEALTH LAW RESEARCH
Elizabeth Adams, Duke University

The following discussion presents the major indexes available in medical libraries. While most are general medical indexes and not specific to health law, the health law researcher who learns to search these indexes will discover a wealth of relevant information.

Index Medicus

Index Medicus is the major index for medical periodical literature. It is published monthly by the National Library of Medicine and cumulates annually. *Index Medicus* indexes more than 3,200 journals in the medical and health-related sciences. Approximately half the citations refer to articles in languages other than English.

Access to *Index Medicus* is by author or subject. Subject headings are assigned by indexers at the National Library of Medicine using a controlled vocabulary of Medical Subject Headings (MeSH). Indexers assign specific subject headings to describe the contents of articles. Four published forms of MeSH help users select appropriate subject headings: an alphabetic list that appears annually in the January issue of *Index Medicus*; an annotated alphabetical list; a tree structure, which is a hierarchical arrangement of the subject headings; and a permeated list. The alphabetic MeSH and annotated alphabetic MeSH provide "translation" from terms that are not subject headings to MeSH and MeSH-related terms. The MeSH tree structure provides a subject categorization of the vocabulary, and is an important tool that helps select terms not easily scanned in the alphabetic MeSH. It is an even more important tool for online computer searching of MEDLINE. The permuted MeSH alphabetically lists each significant word from a subject heading or cross-reference, then lists under each word all the MeSH terms and cross-references used in the thesaurus containing this word. Thus, anyone unfamiliar with the MeSH system can access it without knowledge of the controlled vocabulary.

MEDLINE

In 1965, the National Library of Medicine announced its Medical Literature and Analysis Retrieval System (MEDLARS), a computerized bibliographic retrieval system providing access to the biomedical literature. More than twenty databases are mounted on the NLM system. Of these databases, MEDLINE is the most heavily used and best known. It is the computerized counterpart of *Index Medicus*, and also contains citations appearing in the *Index to Dental Literature* and the *International Nursing Index*.

MEDLINE offers several advantages over the *Index Medicus*. First, the computer can locate information more rapidly and precisely than can manual methods, sorting through thousands of citations quickly. Thus it saves the user valuable time. Second, several search terms can be combined to retrieve only those articles that meet all the user's requirements. A search can be tailored to retrieve all the references available on a topic, or to retrieve only a few "select" references. Third, more search terms are available in MEDLINE than in the printed *Index Medicus*. Citations are printed under one to three headings in *Index Medicus*; up to 20 subject headings per article are available online. Fourth, MEDLINE searching allows the user to find information in ways not available in the printed index, providing access by journal title, language, or words that appear in the title or abstract of the article. As comprehensive as the MeSH vocabulary is, including over 14,000 headings, it still does not include every topic. A MEDLINE search may be entered in the user's own words to search for words appearing in the title or abstract of the article. This capability provides a great deal of flexibility in searching. Another advantage is that references are available in MEDLINE one month before the printed copy of *Index Medicus* is available. *Index Medicus* is produced from the online database. MEDLINE also provides abstracts unavailable in *Index Medicus*. The abstracts often provide enough information to help the user determine whether the complete article should be read.

MEDLINE includes citations from 1966 to the present and is available through the National Library of Medicine, Bibliographic Retrieval Services, Dialog Information Services, and other database vendors.

Hospital Literature Index

Hospital Literature Index is published quarterly by the American Hospital Association in cooperation with the National Library of Medicine. The *Index* covers English-language journal literature in the subject areas of health administration in hospitals, health centers, health maintenance organizations, and other group practice facilities; health planning; organization; economics; legislation; accreditation and licensure; and health insurance.

The present format of *Hospital Literature Index* is similar to *Index Medicus*, with citations listed under subject headings and in the author index. MeSH terms are currently used for subject headings. When searching for citations prior to 1978, Alice Dunlap's *Hospital Literature Subject Headings* (2d ed., 1977, AHA) should be used for subject access to the cumulative indexes. In 1978, *Hospital Literature Subject Headings Transition Guide to Medical Subject Headings* was published by the AHA to aid the change of subject headings. Since MeSH terms are now used in *Hospital Literature Index*, the same broad concepts referred to earlier may be used to cover the legal- and policy-related aspects of health care.

HEALTH File

The online counterpart to *Hospital Literature Index* is the Health Planning and Administration Files (HEALTH), which covers 1975 to the present. The HEALTH file is an online bibliographic database containing citations to the literature dealing with nonclinical aspects of health care delivery. HEALTH is a composite file constructed of citations from nonjournal literature. The Special List Health journals, and citations from nonjournal literature. The Special List Health journals are chosen and indexed by the American Hospital Association. In May 1983, documents cited in the Health Planning Series of the Weekly Government Abstracts supplied by the National Health Planning Information Center (NHPIC) were added to HEALTH. These documents are all English nonjournal publications--mostly technical reports, but also including some monographs, monograph chapters, and theses--dating back to 1975. The citations from MEDLINE include English-, French-, and German-language citations, which make it different from the printed *Hospital Literature Index*, in which only English-language articles appear.

The basic method of searching HEALTH uses MeSH headings. As with MEDLINE, however, textwords play an important part in searching the HEALTH file. MeSH cannot always keep pace with the rapidly changing health care terminology. "Wrongful Birth" is a good example of the need to search by text words.

Since part of the HEALTH file is generated from MEDLINE, the two files overlap. The most cost-effective way to eliminate this overlap is to use the same search terms in each file, searching MEDLINE first. Then combine the HEALTH file retrieval with the Special List indicator and the NHPIC indicator. The result will be the set of HEALTH citations, including the nonjournal NHPIC records, that have not appeared in MEDLINE.

HEALTH is available through the National Library of Medicine, Bibliographic Retrieval Services, and Dialog

Information Services. For a comparison of HEALTH, MEDLINE and HEALTHLAWYER holdings, see Table 1.

BIOETHICSLINE

BIOETHICSLINE is a multidisciplinary file covering the ethical, legal and public policy aspects of medicine, health care, and biomedical and behavioral research. It is produced at the Center for Bioethics, Kennedy Institute of Ethics, Georgetown University, and is made available online through the National Library of Medicine's MEDLARS system. BIOETHICSLINE citations appear in print form in the annual *Bibliography of Bioethics*. The database now contains over 17,000 English-language citations from the literature of law, religion, psychology, philosophy, and the popular media, as well as the health sciences. Included are references to journal and newspaper articles, books, court decisions, bills, state and federal statutes, and audiovisual materials. BIOETHICSLINE is intended to provide comprehensive coverage of all substantive materials on bioethical topics published in English since 1973.

Searching techniques for BIOETHICSLINE are similar to those used for MEDLINE. However, keywords provide the primary means of subject access, so the searcher should first consult the *Bioethics Thesaurus* to determine the most appropriate search terms. Keywords play the same role in searching BIOETHICSLINE that MeSH headings do in MEDLINE, and the Bioethics Thesaurus was developed specifically to reflect the subject interests of the cross-disciplinary field of Bioethics. Searching is done using a combination of MeSH and *Bioethics Thesaurus* terms and textwords from the title of the article.

Excerpta Medica

Excerpta Medica is a major abstracting service containing biomedical and pharmaceutical information taken from more than 4,500 primary medical journals. The abstracts appear in one or more of over forty subject sections, which

Table 1

Comparison of Legal Journals Indexed in *Hospital Literature Index/* HEALTH File/ *Index Medicus*/MEDLINE, and HEALTHLAWYER

	Hospital Literature Index/ File	Index Medicus/ MEDLINE	HEALTH-LAWYER
Acta Medicinae Legalis et Socialis		X	
American Journal of Forensic Medicine and Pathology	X		
American Journal of Law and Medicine	X	X	X
Archiv fur Kriminologie		X	
Beitrage zur Gerichtlichen Medizin		X	
Bulletin of the American Academy of Psychiatry and the Law	X	X	
Cornell Law Review	X		
Duke Law Journal	X		
Employee Relations Journal	X		
Federal Register	X		
Forensic Science International	X	X	
Harvard Law Review	X		
Health Law in Canada	X		
Health Law Vigil	X		
Hospital Law Newsletter			X
International Journal of Law and Psychiatry	X	X	
Journal of Forensic Sciences	X	X	
Journal--Forensic Science Society	X	X	
Journal of Health Politics, Policy and Law	X		X

206

Table 1 Continued

	Hospital Literature Index/ File	Index Medicus/ MEDLINE	HEALTH-LAWYER
Journal of Legal Medicine	X	X	
Journal of Medical Ethics	X	X	X
Labor Law Journal	X		
Law, Medicine and Health Care	X		X
Legal Medicine		X	
Medicine and Law	X	X	
Medicine, Science and the Law	X	X	
Medico-Legal Bulletin		X	
Medico-Legal Journal	X	X	
Michigan Law Review	X		
Nippon Hoigaku Zasshi, Japanese Journal of Legal Medicine		X	
Patient Care Law			X
Population Reports, Series E: Law and Policy		X	
Specialty Law Digest, Health Care Monthly	X		X
Washington Report on Medicine and Health	X		X
Zeitschrift fur Rechtsmedizin, Journal of Legal Medicine		X	

correspond to broad subject areas that often coincide with a traditional medical specialty. A printed publication is produced for each section.

The online *Excerpta Medica* file is called EMBASE. EMBASE represents the entire *Excerpta Medica* file, whereas the printed sections contain only 60 percent of the online file. Editorial policies at *Excerpta Medica* allow each section's editor to determine whether citations in a section are to be included in the printed journal or remain only available online.

The *Excerpta Medica* controlled vocabulary, Master List of Medical Indexing Terms (MALIMET), contains 220,000 preferred terms and 250,000 synonyms. Because of this detailed indexing vocabulary, *Excerpta Medica* is often useful in locating articles on very narrow topics that cannot be as specifically approached in *Index Medicus*/MEDLINE. *Excerpta Medica* also indexes several health law journals that are not covered by either *Index Medicus* or *Hospital Literature Index*. *Excerpta Medica* is available through Bibliographic Retrieval Services from 1980 through the present, and through Dialog Information Services from 1974 to the present.

National Technical Information Service

The National Technical Information Service (NTIS) was established in 1945 as the publication board of the U.S. Department of Commerce. The Service's purpose is to supply copies of unclassified government technical reports. It is the central source for public sale of government-sponsored research and development reports and other analyses prepared by federal agencies, contractors, and grant recipients. More than one million titles are represented in the NTIS database. NTIS holds some data specific to state and local areas that is otherwise difficult to find. This literature can complement the journal literature retrieval from MEDLINE and HEALTH. From its database NTIS generates *Government Reports Announcements and Index*, which is published every two weeks. Every document listed in the database or printed version is available for purchase from NTIS. Many of these documents are also available in the documents departments of academic libraries, which receive them as depository items.

The NTIS database is available through Bibliographic Retrieval Services from 1970 forward, through Dialog Information Services from 1964 forward, and through Systems Development Corporation from 1970 forward.

HEALTHLAWYER
Azike A. Ntephe, American Hospital Association

The American Hospital Association's online library, HEALTHLAWYER^{SM}, is an electronic database designed specifically for health law professionals, including attorneys, hospital administrators, risk managers, and quality assurance personnel. HEALTHLAWYER is devoted entirely to recent developments in health law, and is a flexible and comprehensive listing of bibliographic references to articles from both health-related legal journals and law-related health publications. Full texts of selected publications, abstracts of relevant law review articles, and educational conference materials are also included. HEALTHLAWYER currently contains over 4,000 citations from more than 60 publications, and is updated and enhanced monthly.

Articles can be searched using words from HEALTHLAWYER's thesaurus (a reference guide containing standard vocabulary terms) or by selecting any word or words likely to be found in the records being searched. Users who need detailed instructions are guided through their search with a series of questions and answers. Once the search is initiated, the system searches the entire database for every occurrence of the search words, scanning every field--including title, author, publisher, date, abstract, or text--for any mention of the exact words or topic selected. Users may limit the search to indicate that they are only interested in occurrences in specific fields. When the search is completed, the system indicates the number of citations the search words have retrieved. The user may modify the search strategy to retrieve a more precise or a more comprehensive result, or may display the citations that the initial search has retrieved. The user may choose to look at some or all the citations and/or examine the entire records or specific fields.

In addition to gaining access to the HEALTHLAWYER database, subscribers have direct link to other available files including MEDLINE and Health Planning and Administration, both from the National Library of Medicine; Drug Information Full Text and International Pharmaceutical Abstracts, from the American Society of Hospital Pharmacies; Harvard Business Review/Online, from John Wiley & Sons; and Medical/Psychological Previews, from BRS/Saunders.

HEALTHLAWYER is designed to work on any computer terminal with telecommunications capabilities by simply dialing a local phone number and entering a private password. Since HEALTHLAWYER is a private database, access is available only through the American Hospital Association's Office of Legal Communications.

THE UNIVERSITY OF ALBERTA HEALTH LAW PROJECT
Martin P.J. Kratz

The Health Law Project was established by Ellen Picard, professor of law and medicine at the University of Alberta, with joint funding from the University and from the Alberta Law Foundation. Until 1982, the Project concentrated on the creation and maintenance of a manual indexing system for major cases and articles on health law which would be of interest to the legal and health care professions in Canada. In 1982, the resource materials were placed in a database--the Health Law Digest--at the University of Alberta. The database was designed by Professor Picard with assistance by Martin P.J. Kratz from the Faculty of Computing Services. Using computers made it possible to store more information and made it readily accessible.

A protocol was set up to teach users how to search the database.[1]

The Health Law Digest operates through the Stanford Public Information Retrieval System (SPIRES) which is available on mainframe computers throughout North America. The Digest encompasses four separate databases: CANCASE, COMCASE, USCASE, and ART. CANCASE emphasizes common law jurisdictions in Canada and contains over 2,500 Canadian cases stored in over 1,500 case histories. It also features over 100 unreported Canadian cases. COMCASE contains Commonwealth health law cases from Britain, Australia, and New Zealand drawn primarily from a systematic search of All England Reports. USCASE includes over 40 American cases; negotiations are under way to gain access to several American medical-legal indexing services. ART holds over 2,900 medical-legal articles from national and international journals, including more than 140 unpublished articles. The four databases may be searched using general or specific keywords, or logical combinations of keywords.

The Health Law Project's database and its computer-assisted instruction system are unique in Canada, and provide a resource to the legal profession, health care professionals, and the public. Any inquiries about the Project or the Digest should be directed to Professor Ellen Picard, Faculty of Law, University of Alberta, Edmonton, Canada T6G 2H5.

Notes

1. For a complete description of this endeavor, see M. Kratz, "Introducing Computing Resources to a Faculty of Law," 42 *Computers and Law* 8 (December 1984).

AN OVERVIEW OF HEALTH LAW RESEARCH AND AN ANNOTATED BIBLIOGRAPHY
Richard A. Danner and Claire M. Germain, Duke University

The Literature of Health Law

This analysis and the following bibliography are designed to meet the needs of researchers attempting to locate information in the field of health law. The analysis is written from the perspective of law librarians, but the same information retrieval problems apply to health administrators, hospital and medical counsel, and academic lawyers interested in health law and administration.[1]

As librarians, we perform two major tasks: collection development (i.e., selecting materials for acquisition and retention in our own libraries) and reference/research (i.e., locating and obtaining information from within our library or from other sources). In health law, both of these tasks are sometimes difficult. There is a growing variety of published information sources for health law, which complicates reference work; the field also has shifting boundaries, which makes it hard to define for collection development purposes. As a result, both law librarians and those in the health field who need health law information are now faced with the problem of having to sift through an expanding number of information sources, without any logical organizational scheme to depend on.

Law librarians, like other librarians serving clients with specialized information needs, find that in interdisciplinary fields the literature is diverse and difficult to control, and information often cannot be obtained from familiar sources. The problems posed by the growth of interdisciplinary approaches to legal scholarship and research have long been of concern to academic law librarians.[2] These approaches began to have significant effects on legal research and law library collection-building in the 1960s, a period when growing interest in interdisciplinary studies coincided with an expanding literature and growing library budgets. For legal scholars, a notable event during that decade was the establishment of the Law and Society Association in 1964 and the initial publication in 1966 of that association's journal, *The Law and Society Review*. Other interdisciplinary journals began publication around that time[3] and the application of various techniques and approaches from the social sciences and humanities to the study of law continues to flourish today.

Of course, the longstanding interrelationship between law and medicine predates the legal academic's concern with interdisciplinary studies. The traditional relationship between law and medicine, however, is not interdisciplinary in the same sense as the relationships between law and other disciplines. Whereas the new interdisciplinary approaches typically involve the application of techniques and perspectives from another discipline to the study of law or the analysis of legal documents, the traditional literature of law and medicine is far less theoretical. In order to aid lawyers in arguing points of medical proof, utilizing expert medical witnesses, or otherwise preparing medical cases, a large literature of textbooks, handbooks, and encyclopedic works on medical issues relevant to the legal profession has developed over the years. Much of this literature is highly practical. It is also highly marketable; some sources have estimated that up to 80 percent of the average lawyer's cases involve some kind of medical questions.[4] Although these traditional materials relating law and medicine remain within the scope of the health law specialist, they no longer encompass all topics we now consider to be part of health law, and their effect on the literature is not really interdisciplinary.

Interdisciplinary approaches have their major effects on the processes of legal scholarship; they signal a move in the academic lawyer's research techniques away from strict doctrinal analysis and toward the use of techniques and research materials from other disciplines.[5] For law librarians and others concerned with supplying the information needed for this sort of research, new expertise in selecting materials from non-law disciplines and facility with indexing and searching tools outside those traditionally used in legal research are required.

The growth and complexity of the health law literature is also due to the need for health law attorneys, health care administrators, and other health care professionals to be aware of the effects of federal and state legislation and regulation. Since World War II, if not before, health care has become a major concern of public policy. With the passage of the Public Health Service Act in 1944,[6] the Hill-Burton Amendments in 1946,[7] the Medicaid amendments in 1965,[8] and other legislation, the impact of federal policy decisions on health care has grown enormously. And where policy is made on the state or national level, the importance of legal considerations increases. Policy decisions are shaped to the ways of existing law, and they create new law in their wake. Since the mid-twentieth century, there has been significant federal policy-making on funding for health research, on health-care organization, and on delivery of health-care services, and a corresponding growth in both legislation and regulation in each of these areas. This growth has created a need for continuing information regarding the factors going into policy-making, and on the impact of policies already in place.

Some policy areas affect health law directly through enacted legislation and regulation. Policy questions also are involved in newly developing areas of concern, such as ethical issues in treatment, bioethics, genetics and human reproduction, and transplantation--whether or not society's concerns have yet been expressed in legislation. The growing importance of health policy considerations to medical and health counsel, other specialists in medical law, and health care administrators has been a major factor in the mushrooming of what we now call health law.

This change to a greater concern with the making of policy decisions and their impact is seen in the changing foci of the standard texts in hospital law and health care law. The early treatments, beginning with Lapp and Ketcham's 1926 text *Hospital Law*[9] and extending through Emanuel and Lillian Hayt's series of texts in the 1940s[10] deal with subjects such as the differences in immunity and liability among charitable, public and private hospitals; the evidentiary value of medical records; the hospital's property rights and corporate status; and organization of the hospital staff. The modern texts, as David Warren pointed out in a recent comparative review, are much more diverse in their coverage.[11] The works he reviewed include several texts aimed at health administrators, and three law school case books. The case books consist largely of excerpted cases, statutes, and other materials, compiled for use as teaching materials in law school courses in law and medicine. Indeed titles of two of the books reviewed are *Cases and Materials on Law and Medicine*[12] the third is entitled *Law, Medicine and Forensic Science*.[13] His review of the coverage of these case books is helpful in showing the changing concerns of the lawyer interested in law and medicine or in health law.

The contemporary works, despite their continued emphasis on and coverage of the conventional medical legal topics--forensic science, medical proof in litigation, medical and hospital liability--also (to varying degrees) cover the broader concerns of health law and policy expressed in government regulation of health care, and the newer areas of policy concern mentioned above. From examining these texts, one gets a sense of the amorphous nature of the field. The same feeling results from an examination of the coverage of the newsletters and journals identified in our own bibliography. Some current periodicals specialize in the traditional concerns of law and medicine, others in specific areas of contemporary concern, and still others in news of government actions and proposals for action; and many provide various combinations of these approaches. The literature of the field is made complex by the variety of its topics, the dispersed sources for the information, and the changing nature of the topics it encompasses.

Another reason why the literature of health law is difficult to work with is the variety of audiences at which it is aimed and marketed. In law generally, librarians have a choice among books and journals aimed directly at the law school market--scholarly monographs and reviews or student decisions are more complicated, because the standard texts have been written not for the lawyer at all, but for the health administrator. The case books, by their nature, do not provide the expository treatment of the field that a treatise does; and there are as yet no book-length treatises or texts designed for the health lawyer, as there are in other areas of law. Perhaps this is because health law is an interdisciplinary field, or because it is a field characterized by the impact of policy considerations; in a field with shifting boundaries, the writing of a standard work may be slow in coming. There does seem to be an increasing concern with legal scholarship in health law, however, as signaled by the starting of two new law-school-based journals in health law.[14]

The literature of texts in health law aimed at health administrators extends from the early treatises in hospital law by the Hayts and others to several recent textbooks.[15] These books all to some extent explain basic principles and institutions of law to their non-lawyer audience, and show how legal principles apply to health law problems. They do not provide, however, the level of analysis and the detailed references to primary sources of the typical treatise written for the lawyer.[16]

The monographic literature of health law is similarly difficult for a law librarian to evaluate, because none of it is totally satisfactory for the professional audience. Little of it is aimed at the academic lawyer or even at the practicing attorney specializing in the area. And while the periodical and current-awareness literature of the field, on the other hand, is aimed at the specialist attorney as well as at the health care professional, there is so much of it, and it is so extremely specialized in coverage and audience, that selection and evaluation decisions are difficult.

The following bibliography provides a perspective on the wealth of information available in that segment of the literature, and on the current resources for organizing and indexing it. The bibliography also illustrates the problems of obtaining information in the field of health law, at the same time that it provides a guide to that information. No bibliography of health law materials can solve the problems we have discussed here: that the field itself is without formal definition, encompassing traditional areas of concern in law and medicine, and in hospital law, as well as new concerns raised by policy considerations in the health care field; that health law lacks the grounding provided by standard legal texts and journals; and that the periodical literature of the field is highly specialized and fragmented, is issued from a number of sources, and is aimed in large part at segments of a broader audience with health law concerns but without legal expertise. In brief, the literature of health law is a literature in need of control, so that information can be located efficiently and effectively. The bibliography we provide is meant as a first step in that direction.

USING THE BIBLIOGRAPHY AS A FIRST STEP

Our bibliography explores the variety of information sources which may be of use to the health law researcher. It more specifically focuses on the important question of access to the materials. The fragmentation of resources and the interdisciplinary nature of the field mandate that the researcher use a multiplicity of indexes to get access to the materials needed. The bibliography describes the various indexes available, and the publications indexed by each. The information sources are available in printed form, as well as in computerized formats, but online search is stressed here.

The bibliography is divided into two main parts: "General Materials" and "Specialized Materials." It is important to understand that the easiest way to get access to the wide range of articles is to use some of the major general indexes to the periodical literature of law, medicine, or health sciences. This is because health law touches upon areas that are not comprehensively covered in the more specialized materials. In addition to subjects classically associated with health law--such as hospital law, medical malpractice, and bioethics--the field currently extends to several other branches of law, including antitrust law and business association (hospital mergers, corporate practice of medicine, HMOs), contracts and torts, patent law, environmental law, and even federal election law (for example, in the context of PACs acting on behalf of the American Hospital Association). Another often overlooked source of information is the bulk of materials published by the government. The list of specialized materials is representative, rather than exhaustive. It takes into consideration the publications of the most important professional associations and interest groups associated with health law. The publisher's information included with each entry should give the reader an idea of the audience contemplated by the publication.

An intelligent research strategy will depend on the research needs to be met. A specialized newsletter might adequately fill the needs of a practicing attorney to keep abreast of current developments. For in-depth research, a computerized literature search through the major periodical indexes will be recommended. Health law researchers would be well-advised to seek the professional services which can be found in medical and law libraries, as well as U.S. depository libraries. Most reference law librarians are well-trained, as well as library-educated. Medical librarians have a strong and well-established tradition of performing computerized literature searches for their patrons. The best place to find government documents is to go to the nearest U.S. government depository library --there is usually one at every university. The main problem with federal documents is that the materials are usually not represented in the main card catalog of the institution. Federal documents librarians, however, have expertise and knowledge of appropriate special indexes and how to use them.

In all these libraries, the staff can be helpful in identifying publications, providing publishers' addresses, explaining the library's resources and services, and if need be, performing computerized literature searches.

Two specialized libraries offer services to their members. The Sagall Library of Law, Medicine and Health Care serves as an information clearinghouse for members of the American Society of Law and Medicine. It is located, together with the executive offices of the Society, in the Law Tower Building of Boston University. Members of the Society may borrow books, use the photocopy services, and get research assistance from the Library. For more information, write to American Society of Law and Medicine, 765 Commonwealth Avenue, Boston, Mass. 02215.

In a similar way, the American Hospital Association sponsors a Resource Center which uses the facilities of the Asa S. Bacon Memorial Library and uses the computerized Health Planning and Administration Database. It provides services to health care specialists. Some are free of charge and others are offered on a fee-for-service basis to both members and nonmembers. Services include factual information, research assistance, and a document delivery service. For more information, write to American Hospital Association Resource Center, 840 Lake Shore Drive, Chicago, Ill. 60611; (312) 280-6263.

Notes

1. Other related bibliographies include: James T. Zigenfuss, *Law, Medicine & Health Care: A Bibliography* (New York: Facts on File, 1984); Salvatore F. Fiscina et al., *A Sourcebook for Research in Law and Medicine* (Owings Mills,, Md.: National Health Publishing, 1985); Lisa Baker, "Health Care Law Information Sources: An Annotated Bibliography," *Legal Reference Services Quarterly* 3 (Fall 1983):3-37.
2. See Mathew F. Dee, "Law Library Purchasing in an Interdisciplinary Era," *Law Library Journal* 63 (1970):19-27; Albert Brecht, "Changes in Legal Scholarship and Their Impact on Law School Library Reference Services," *Law Library Journal* 77 (1984-85):157-64.
3. Examples include: the *Columbia Journal of Law & Social Problems* (1965 on); the *New York University Review of Law and Social Change* (1971 on); the University of Chicago's *Journal of Legal Studies* (1972 on); the *Journal of Psychiatry and Law* (1973 on); and the University of Utah's *Journal of Contemporary Law* (1974 on). Duke's *Law and Contemporary Problems* started

publication in 1933, and the University of Chicago's *Journal of Law and Economics* in 1958.
4. William A. Curran and E. Donald Shapiro, *Law, Medicine, and Forensic Science*, 2d ed. (Boston: Little, Brown, 1970), p. viii.
5. See Brecht, "Changes in Legal Scholarship," pp. 158-59.
6. 58 Stat. 682, 42 U.S.C. sec. 201 et seq. (1982).
7. Hospital Survey and Construction Act, 60 Stat. 1040 (1946).
8. Health Insurance for the Aged Act, 79 Stat. 290 (1965).
9. John A. Lapp and Dorothy Ketcham, *Hospital Law* (Milwaukee: Bruce, 1926).
10. See Emanuel Hayt and Lillian R. Hayt, *Legal Aspects of Hospital Practices* (New York: Hospital Textbook Co., 1938); *Legal Guide for American Hospitals* (New York: Hospital Textbook Co., 1940); *Law of Hospital, Physician and Patient* (New York: Hospital Textbook Co., 1947).
11. See David G. Warren, "The Coming of Age of Health Law: An Examination of Recent Textbooks," *Journal of Health Politics, Policy and Law* 8 (Summer 1983): 387-95. See also David G. Warren, review of *Law, Science and Medicine* by Judith Areen et al. in *The Journal of Legal Medicine* 6 (June 1985):271-81.
12. David J. Sharpe, Salvatore F. Fiscina, and Murdock Head, *Cases and Materials on Law and Medicine* (St. Paul: West, 1978); Walter Wadlington, Jon R. Waltz, and Roger B. Dworkin, *Cases and Materials on Law and Medicine* by Judith Areen et al. in *The Journal of Legal Medicine* 6 (June 1985):271-81.
13. William J. Curran and E. Donald Shapiro, *Law, Medicine, and Forensic Science*, 3d ed. (Boston: Little, Brown, 1982).
14. They are Cleveland-Marshall College of Law's *Journal of Law and Health* (1985 on) and Catholic University Law School's *Journal of Contemporary Health Law and Policy* (1985 on).
15. Among the current texts are: Tom Christoffel, *Health and the Law* (New York: The Free Press, 1982); George D. Pozgar, *Legal Aspects of Health Care Administration* (Germantown, Md.: Aspen, 1979); Robert D. Miller,

Problems in Hospital Law, 4th ed. (Rockville, Md.: Aspen, 1983); Kenneth R. Wing, *The Law and the Public's Health*, 2d ed. (Ann Arbor: Health Administration Press, 1985); Michael C. MacDonald, Kathryn C. Meyer, and Beth Essig, *Health Care Law: A Practical Guide* (New York: Matthew Bender, 1985).

16. Perhaps the closest approximation in health to the standard legal treatise in other fields is Aspen System, Corporation, *Hospital Law Manual*, 6 vols. (Rockville, Md.: Aspen, 1983 on). The set has three volumes written for the health administrator and three for attorneys. Neither part goes far beyond the traditional concerns of hospital law.

I. General Materials

INDEXES TO PERIODICAL LITERATURE

Indexes to Legal Periodicals

Current Law Index or *Legal Resource Index* (microfilm). Belmont, Calif.: Information Access Corporation, 1980 on. Monthly, with cumulations.
This is the best and most comprehensive source for current information. Over 700 English-language law periodicals are indexed, including the U.S., British, Canadian, Australian, and New Zealand legal literature and several U.S. legal newspapers, such as *American Lawyer*, *Legal Times*, and *National Law Journal*. It is limited to periodicals, however, and does not cover digests and specialized newsletters. It is available in paper format and cumulative microfilm. A new version is *Legal Trac*, the database being stored on a videodisc and access provided through an IBM-PC. The *Index* can also be searched online.

Index to Legal Periodicals. Bronx, N.Y.: Wilson Co., 1908 on. Quarterly, with annual cumulations.
Forerunner to *CLI/LRI*. Also searchable online via "Wilsonline."

Index to Foreign Legal Periodicals. Berkeley, Calif.: University of California Press, 1960 on. Quarterly, with cumulations.
Provides access to the world legal periodical literature, mainly in languages other than English.

Index to Periodical Articles Related to Law. Dobbs Ferry, N.Y.: Glanville Publications, 1959 on. Quarterly.

Index to Canadian Legal Periodical Literature. Montreal, Que.: Index to Canadian Legal Periodical Literature, 1961 on. Quarterly.
Covers some periodicals not indexed by *CLI/LRI*.

Indexes to Medical and Health Sciences Periodicals

Hospital Literature Index. Chicago, Ill.: American Hospital Association, 1945 on. Quarterly, with annual cumulations.
Indexes the English-language literature dealing with the nonclinical aspects of health care delivery, including health insurance, HMOs, and financial and personnel management. Cooperatively produced with the National Library of Medicine and currently developed from the *Health Planning and Administration* online database.

Index Medicus. Bethesda, Md.: National Library of Medicine, 1960 on. Monthly with annual cumulations.
Comprehensive index to every area in the broad field of biomedicine. Covers approximately 2600 periodicals in all languages. Derived from MEDLINE online database which also corresponds to the printed indexes, *Index to Dental Literature* and *International Nursing Index*.

General Indexes

A variety of interdisciplinary indexes, such as *Public Affairs Information Service* and the *New York Times Index*, may be of use to the health law researcher for articles written in periodicals, magazines, and newspapers outside of the medico-legal field. Most are searchable online.

Access to Government Information

Statistical

The following two major commercial indexes stand out because of their comprehensiveness. Both are searchable online.

American Statistics Index (ASI). Bethesda, Md.: Congressional Information Service, 1974 on. Monthly, with quarterly and annual cumulations.
Indexes and abstracts over 500 sources within the federal government (e.g., statistics from the National Center for Health Statistics).

Statistical Reference Index (SRI). Bethesda, Md.: Congressional Information Service, 1981 on. Monthly, with quarterly and annual cumulations.
Indexes and abstracts sources from U.S. private organizations, such as the American Medical Association, and state government agencies.

Congressional

Congressional Information Service (CIS). Bethesda, Md.: Congressional Information Service, 1970 on. Monthly, with quarterly and annual cumulations.
Indexes and abstracts all congressional publications, including hearings, reports, prints, and documents. Also searchable online.

General

Monthly Catalog. Washington, D.C.: G.P.O., 1985 on. Monthly, with cumulations.
General index to all U.S. documents distributed by the Government Printing Office. Can also be searched online.

MEDOC. Salt Lake City, Utah: University of Utah Health Sciences Library, 1975 on. Quarterly, with annual cumulations.

Index to U.S. government publications in the medical and health sciences.

CIS Federal Register Index. Bethesda, Md.: Congressional Information Service. Most comprehensive index to the *Federal Register*, which contains rules and regulations of the federal executive and administrative agencies, as well as proposed rules and notices. Rules and regulations having a general applicability are at the end of the year codified into the *Code of Federal Regulations*. Both the *Federal Register* and the *Code of Federal Regulations* can be searched online.

Government Reports Announcements and Index. Springfield, Va.: National Technical Information Service. Biweekly. This is the main index to National Technical Information Service documents. It provides access to research, reports, and studies produced under federal grants and contracts. Numerous health law topics can also be found.

LEXIS and WESTLAW

LEXIS and WESTLAW are the two major full-text computerized legal retrieval systems. They both consist of various libraries containing cases, administrative decisions, attorney general opinions, regulatory and other materials, now including law reviews.

WESTLAW does not contain any specific health law database. Their Office of Research and Development does not have any plans for a specialized database. Specific West Digest topics, such as "Social Security" and "Health Law and Environment," can be used to narrow down a search.

LEXIS also does not have a specific health law database. However, other services are available in addition to LEXIS, such as NEXIS and MEDIS. NEXIS contains the full text of over 100 publications, including the newspapers, magazines, wire services, newsletters, and reference materials. It is especially useful for information on new products and drugs, pending lawsuits, trends, and statistics. MEDIS is a new service and consists of over 50 clinical medical publications, journals, newsletters, and textbooks, comprising the full range of medical practice. The health law researcher might use it to determine standards of care, identify potential expert witnesses, gain background information on a medical topic, and generally to monitor trends in health care.

II. Specialized Materials

The variety of publications can be broken down into the following categories: major periodicals, digests of primary sources (legislation, regulations, and case law), and newsletters. These come from many sources, including the academic community, professional associations, and interest groups, as well as the government. The list is representative. To it could be added the numerous newsletters of the Health Law Sections of the State Bar Associations--e.g., the *Health Law News*, published quarterly by the California Society of Health Care Attorneys. Only a few private law firm newsletters are mentioned here.

Major Periodicals

American Journal of Law and Medicine. Boston, Mass.: American Society of Law and Medicine, Inc., 1975 on. Quarterly. $40. Indexed in *Current Contents, Excerpta Medica*, HEALTH-LAWYER, *Hospital Literature Index, Index Medicus, SSCI, Index to Legal Periodicals, CLI*.

Health Law in Canada. Scarborough, Ont.: Butterworth, 1980 on. Quarterly. $45. Indexed in *CLI, Hospital Literature Index* and *Index to Canadian Periodical Literature*. Published for the Canadian Institute of Law and Medicine.

Journal of Contemporary Health Law and Policy. Washington, D.C.: Catholic University of America, 1985 on. Annual. $10.

Journal of Law and Health. Cleveland, Ohio: Cleveland-Marshall College of Law, 1985 on. Semiannual. $15.

Journal of Legal Medicine. Long Island City, N.Y.: American College of Legal Medicine, 1979 on. Quarterly. $56. Indexed in *CLI*, *ILP*, *Hospital Literature Index*, and *Index Medicus/ MEDLINE*.

Journal of Medical Ethics. London: Professional and Scientific Publications, 1975 on. Quarterly. $58. Indexed in *Current Contents*, *Excerpta Medica*, HEALTHLAWYER, and *Index Medicus*.

Law, Medicine and Health Care. Boston, Mass.: American Society of Law and Medicine, 1973 on. 6 times a year. $40. Indexed in *CLI*, HEALTHLAWYER, and *Hospital Literature Index*. Continues *Medico-Legal News* (1973-1981) and *Nursing Law and Ethics*.

Legal Medical Quarterly. Toronto, Ont.: Legal Medical Quarterly, 1977 on. Quarterly. $40. Indexed in *CLI*.

Medical Trial Technique Quarterly. Wilmette, Ill.: Callaghan, 1980 on. Quarterly. $73.50. Indexed in *CLI*.

Topics in Hospital Law. Rockville, Md.: Aspen Systems, 1985 on. Quarterly. $59.50.

Digests

Bioethics Reporter. Frederick, Md.: University Publications of America, 1983 on. Monthly. $500.
Subject reporter containing cases, articles, and legislation concerning ethical and legal issues in medicine, health care administration, and human experimentation.

The Citation: A Medicolegal Digest for Physicians. Chicago, Ill.: American Medical Association. Twice monthly. $40. Contains case briefs in all areas of medicine.

Health Law Bulletin. Chapel Hill, N.C.: Institute of Government, University of North Carolina. Irregular. $2/issue. Focuses on North Carolina law (legislation and cases) relating to public health, mental health, medicine, and hospitals, as well as medical-legal investigations and medical jurisprudence.

Health Law Digest. Washington, D.C.: National Health Lawyers Association, 1971 on. Monthly. Free to members, $150 to nonmembers. Indexed in HEALTHLAWYER.
Contains annotations of cases related to health care. Arranged by subject, such as antitrust, constitutional law, medical records, and health planning. Heavily relied upon by health care lawyers.

Hospital Law. Chicago, Ill.: American Academy of Hospital Attorneys of the American Hospital Association. Monthly. Indexed in HEALTHLAWYER.
Discusses recent court decisions affecting hospitals.

International Digest of Health Legislation. Geneva, Switzerland: World Health Organization, 1949 on. Quarterly. $60. Indexed in *Biological Abstracts*.
Covers health laws, regulations, and studies in comparative health legislation.

Malpractice Digest. St. Paul, Minn.: St. Paul Fire and Marine Insurance, 4 times a year. Free.
Published for the medical liability insurance policy holders.

Medical Liability Reporter. San Francisco, Calif.: Litigation Research Group, 1979 on. Monthly. $192.
Summarizes and analyzes recent decisions of national significance for the health care law practice, thoroughly indexed. Continues in part *Professional Liability Reporter.*

Reporter on Human Reproduction and the Law. Boston, Mass.: Legal-Medical Studies, 1971 on. Bimonthly. $55.
Contains cases, statutes, and materials on law and life sciences.

Specialty Law Digest: Health Care Cases. Blaine, Minn.: Specialty Digest Publications, 1985 on. Monthly, annual cumulation. $290. ($266 renewal). Formerly published by Bureau of National Affairs. Indexed in HEALTHLAWYER and

Hospital Literature Index. Includes case annotations, bibliographies, and commentaries, usually a reprint of a law review article.

Newsletters

Action Kit for Hospital Law. Pittsburgh, Pa.: Horty, Springer & Mattern. Law firm newsletter.

Biomedical Safety and Standards Newsletter. Brea, Calif.: Quest, 1971 on. Twice a month. $98.
Written for the fields of medical safety and standards. Includes factual reports on safety hazards and product recalls, standards, legal actions, legislation and regulations, hospital safety, education, and meetings.

Concern for Dying. New York, N.Y.: Concern for Dying, 1975 on. Quarterly. Free to hospitals and school libraries; others $5.
Contains articles on subjects such as living wills and the right to refuse life support.

Developments in Mental Health Law. Charlottesville, Va.: Institute of Law, Psychiatry and Public Policy at the University of Virginia. Quarterly. Free.
Analyzes current national and state (primarily Virginia) developments in the legislature and courts.

Faculty Practice Quarterly. Washington, D.C.: National Health Lawyers Association, 1984/85 on. Quarterly.
This newsletter was "created to respond to the particular needs of professionals involved with faculty practice plans and related legal matters."

Health Advocate. Los Angeles, Calif.: National Health Law Program, 1982 on. Quarterly. $15.

Health Care Briefing. Los Angeles, Calif.: Arthur Young, 1977 on. *Health Law Bulletin.* See above under "Digests."

Health Law Outlook. Philadelphia, Pa.: Wood, Lucksinger and Epstein. Monthly. Law firm newsletter.

Health Law Update. Philadelphia, Pa.: Wolf, Block, Schorr and Solis-Cohen, 1984 on. Quarterly. Free to clients. Law firm newsletter.

Health Law Vigil. Chicago, Ill.: American Hospital Association, Office of Legal and Regulatory Affairs, 1980 on. Every two weeks. $150, members; $200, nonmembers. Indexed in HEALTHLAWYER, *Hospital Literature Index*, and MEDLINE. Analyzes judicial, legislative, and regulatory developments affecting hospitals.

The Health Lawyer. Chicago, Ill.: American Bar Association, Forum Committee on Health Law, 1984 on. 3-4 times a year. Free to members.
Contains substantive articles and committee news.

Health Lawyers News Report. Washington, D.C.: National Health Lawyers Association, 1973 on. Monthly. Free to members, $34 nonmembers.
Reports on mainly legislative and administrative developments in the health care field.

HealthSpan. Clifton, N.J.: Law and Business Inc., 1985 on. 10 times a year. $95.
Covers several health-related areas (e.g., bioethics, reimbursements, professional issues). Continues *HealthScan*.

Health Services Information. Washington, D.C.: Healthcare Publications, 1973 on. Weekly. $275.
Reports on health policy and cost containment, including legislation and court decisions.

Henry P. Kaplan Newsletter. 20745 Sevilla Lane, Saratoga, Calif. 95070. Law firm newsletter.

Highlights. Washington, D.C.: National Institutes of Health, Division of Legislative Analysis.
Reviews congressional action regarding health matters that affects NIH.

Hospital Ethics. Chicago, Ill.: American Hospital Association, 1985 on. Bimonthly. $60 for members, $80 for nonmembers. Indexed in HEALTHLAWYER.
Contains news on human experimentation, care of the dying and newborn, behavioral ethics, and other aspects of hospital ethics.

Hospital Law Manual Newsletter. Attorney's Edition. Germantown, Md.: Health Law Center, Aspen Systems Corp. Separately numbered section of *Hospital Law Manual*.

Hospital Law Newsletter. Rockville, Md.: Aspen Systems Corp., 1983 on. Monthly. $140. Indexed in HEALTHLAWYER.
Reviews recent legal developments. Also contains substantive articles.

Hospital Week. Chicago, Ill.: American Hospital Publishing, 1964 on. Weekly. $20.
Covers national and local health-care-related developments of interest to hospital administrators. Includes cases and legislation.

Infection Control Digest. Chicago, Ill.: American Hospital Association, 1979 on. Monthly. Indexed in HEALTHLAWYER.
Discusses vaccines, infectious diseases, and related topics.

Lawyers' Medical Digest. Wilmette, Ill.: Callaghan, 1984 on. Monthly. $125.
Digest of articles from leading medical journals of interest to attorneys handling medical-related cases.

Legal Aspects of Medical Practice. Long Island City, N.Y.: American Society of Law and Medicine, 1972 on. Monthly. $48. Indexed in *CLI*, *Index Medicus*.
Each issue contains two or three articles, a question-and-answer column, and book reviews.

Legal Memorandum. Chicago, Ill.: AHA, Office of Legal and Regulatory Affairs, 1985 on. Monthly.

Medicaid Fraud Report. Washington, D.C.: National Association of Attorneys General, 1981 on. Monthly. $95.
State litigation in Medicaid fraud.

Medical Benefits. Charlottesville, Va.: Kelly Communications, 1984 on. Every 2 weeks. $112.
A medical-economics digest. Includes excerpts from newspapers and magazines.

Medical Devices, Diagnostics and Instrumentation Reports --"The Gray Sheet." Chevy Chase, Md.: F-D-C Reports, Inc., 1974 on. Weekly. $300. Indexed in *Pharmaceutical News Index* and *MEDIS*.
In-depth coverage of medical devices--regulatory agency and congressional news, industry news, etc.

Medical Liability Advisory Service. Arlington, Va.: Capitol Publications, Inc., 1977 on. Monthly. $96.
Covers litigation, case law, government regulation, and insurance trends in medical malpractice.

Medical Liability Monitor. Glencoe, Ill.: Malpractice Lifeline Inc., 1975 on. Semimonthly. $97.
Formerly *Malpractice Lifeline*. Deals exclusively with the problems and trends of medical professional liability.

Medical Malpractice Law & Strategy. New York, N.Y.: Leader Publications, Inc., 1983 on. Monthly. $135.
Medical articles by physicians, dentists, and nurses; includes strategies for cases, legislative and judicial developments.

Medical Malpractice Verdicts, Settlements and Experts. Nashville, Tenn.: L. Smith Publishing, 1985 on. Monthly. $197.
A malpractice jury verdict reporter.

Medical Mutual Insurance Newsletter. Raleigh, N.C.: Medical Mutual Insurance Company of N.C. Quarterly.
Highlights activities and services of the insurance company.

Medical Staff News. Chicago, Ill.: American Hospital Publishing, 1971 on. Monthly. $18. Indexed in HEALTHLAWYER. Briefs hospital physicians and administrators on issues such as professional liability, joint-venturing hospitals, and legal aspects of organ requests for transplantation.

Medicare Medicaid Information. Washington, D.C.: Healthcare Publications, 1974 on. Every two weeks. $150.
Covers legislative developments and HHS news dealing with Medicare and Medicaid.

Medico-Legal Bulletin. Richmond, Va.: Virginia State Health Department, Office of the Chief Medical Examiner and Medical College of Virginia, Department of Legal Medicine, 1951 on. Bimonthly. Free to qualified personnel. Indexed in *Index Medicus, Excerpta Medica*.
Contains articles of interest to health and health law practitioners.

Member's Page. Washington, D.C.: National Health Lawyers Association, 1985 on.
Columns in this newsletter include the President's Corner, job vacancies, and NHLA members developments.

Mental and Physical Disability Law Reporter. Washington, D.C.: American Bar Association, Committee on Mentally Disabled, 1976 on. 6 times a year. $135, institutions; $90, individuals. Indexed in *CLI*.
Covers all aspects of law for the handicapped--case law, administrative actions, legislation, bibliographies, etc.

NCHSR Program Note. Rockville, Md.: National Center for Health Services Research and Health Care Technology Assessment.

Physician Law Notes. Greenville, N.C.: East Carolina University School of Medicine, 1982 on. Monthly.

Prognosis. Raleigh, N.C.: N.C. Bar Association Health Law Section; N.C. Society of Health Care Attorneys, 1985 on. Quarterly. Free to organization members.

Regan Report on Hospital Law. Providence, R.I.: Medica Press, 1960 on. Monthly. $32.
Covers federal and state decisions on medical issues.

Risk Management Foundation Forum. Cambridge, Mass.: Harvard Medical Institutions, Inc. Bimonthly. Free to institutions, staff, and physicians associated with Risk Management Foundation. Includes articles on subjects relative to hospital risk management.

Risk Review. Raleigh, N.C.: North Carolina Hospital Association. Monthly. Discusses cases and legislation concerning malpractice and negligence.

State Health Legislation Report. Chicago, Ill.: American Medical Association, Public Affairs Group, Division of Legislative Activities, Department of State Legislation. Monthly.
Reports on recent state actions in the area of health law.

State Health Reports on Mental Health, Alcoholism and Drug Abuse. Washington, D.C.: Office of Research and Demonstrations, Health Care Financing Administration. Irregular.
Covers mental health, alcoholism, and drug abuse.

Washington Memo. Washington, D.C.: American Hospital Association. Weekly. $250. Indexed in HEALTHLAWYER.
Weekly report on federal legislative and administrative activities.

Washington Report on Health Legislation and Regulation. Indexed in HEALTHLAWYER.

Washington Report on Medicine and Health. Washington, D.C.: McGraw-Hill, 1975 on. Weekly. $367. Indexed in *Hospital Literature Index*.

Computerized Indexing/Abstracting Services

HEALTHLAWYER. Chicago, Ill.: Office of Legal Communications of the American Hospital Association.

Bibliographic database devoted to recent developments in health law. Contains case digests, full text of articles from selected newsletters, and abstracts from articles in law reviews, journals, and conference proceedings.

Health Law Project. University of Alberta, Edmonton, Canada. Supported by a grant from the Alberta Foundation.
Contains Canadian, English, and Commonwealth cases dealing with health law issues, as well as articles from major Canadian and American medical-legal journals and other materials.

PRINTED BY PERMISSION OF THE DUKE UNIVERSITY PRESS FROM THE *JOURNAL OF HEALTH POLITICS, POLICY AND LAW*, Vol. 11, No. 1, Spring 1986, copyright 1986 by Duke University.